BUILD YOU

The new marketing manifesto for restaurants, bars and cafés

SUSANNE CURRID

Build Your Tribe
The new marketing manifesto for restaurants, bars and cafés

First published in 2013 by

Panoma Press
48 St Vincent Drive, St Albans, Herts, AL1 5SJ, UK

info@panomapress.com
www.panomapress.com

Book layout by Neil Coe

Printed on acid-free paper from managed forests. This book is printed on demand to fulfill orders, so no copies will be remaindered or pulped.

ISBN 978-1-909623-13-2

For Holly

BOOK REVIEWS

"This book fills an important gap by offering practical advice to restaurant and pub owners everywhere about how to promote their venues."

Luke Johnson, CEO Patisserie Valerie and The Draft House and former CEO PizzaExpress

"An essential read for anybody in hospitality who is writing a marketing plan."

James Nolan, ex Operations Director, Towercrest Enterprises

"A very good, clearly written and thoroughly comprehensive 'how to' handbook for today's hospitality business that I will certainly be referring to frequently."

Debbie Pearce, Restaurant Marketing Consultant and Director, Fork Off Management

"A must have marketing book for anyone aiming for enduring success in the leisure industry"

Gian Luca Scanu, General Manager, Monikers Hoxton Square

ACKNOWLEDGMENTS

I owe so much gratitude and thanks to the following friends, family, colleagues, communities, clients and mentors who have provided me with fantastic support, inspiration and feedback in the development of this book and my business.

Jo Kruczynska, Tony McKinlay, Sarita McKinlay, Jo Middleton, James Nolan, Kieran Hall, Gian Luca Scanu, Debbie Pearce, Mads Nybo Jorgenson, Susie Collings, Brian Tennent, Patrick Blunt, Yohannes Bitowlign, Simon Isaac, Gilead Yeffett, Jean-Michel Orieux, Fabricio Aguilar, Carine Munch, Lesley Ellard, Cormac Heron, Nick O'Doherty, Surekha Aggarwal, Gerry Dawson, Brendan Treacy, Aidan Treacy, Shaun & Victoria Adams, Sharon Bambaji, Lisa Kosky, Clare Conway, Dominco Arenare, Andrew & Debbie Swainson, Gary Rodgers , Elaine Bowman, Donna McKoy, Tom Maddocks, Terri George, Jill & Derek Dann, Tim Prizeman, Viv Grant, Claudia Crawley, Graham Ogilvie, Karen & Philip Paterson, Sonia Brown MBE, Jenny and David Cruickshank, my KPI accountability group buddies, Sean

Toal, Paul Higgs, Linda Everett, Michael Gerd Ehlert, Ben MacLoughlin, Louise Walker, Ricardo Lopez, Onur Ibrahim and Sammy Blindell, my KPI tutors Daniel Priestley, Andrew Priestley, Mindy Gibbins-Klein, Nic Rixson, Shaa Wasmund, Penny Power, Mike Harris, all the wonderful ladies of Athena London, my brilliant proof reader and friend Yvette Jane, Patricia Rayner for her fantastic photography, Myla and Davis in Herne Hill, the team at Panoma Press, all my family in Ireland, most especially my amazing grandmother, Katherine Mallin, my mother and father who's love and support gave me the best possible start in life and my sister Grainne and my brother David who've always been there for me.

If I have forgotten to mention you, please know that your help and support is very much appreciated.

And last, but definitely not least, I'd like to thank my partner Victor who's given me so much wonderful love, encouragement and support over the last five years. Without you, none of this would have come into being. I thank you with the deepest, heart-felt gratitude.

CONTENTS

Chapter 3 - Your Marketing Plan 51

Chapter 4 - Connect With your Tribe on the Internet 73

Chapter 5 - Attract Visiting Customers to your Tribe   99

Chapter 6 - Your Marketing Dream Team   119

Chapter 7 - Which Social Media Channels?   133

Chapter 8 - Your Essential Digital Marketing Tools   161

Chapter 9 - Getting Results   175

References   191

About the Author   193

INTRODUCTION

This book is for anyone who takes an active part in the marketing of a restaurant, bar, pub or café business. Whatever size your business, whether you're working for a large fast casual chain, a gourmet fine dining establishment or you're a plucky entrepreneur who's just launched a new pub & restaurant, my aim is to open your eyes to a new way of marketing your business.

The big buzz these days in marketing is all about social media. With vast numbers of people jumping online to tell friends, family and the wider Internet about their latest food and drink experience, it's become essential that businesses know how to join in with these conversations. However, the social experience of sharing our news and opinions is not just confined to the Internet. I believe a successful marketing strategy will work with ALL those points where people interact and come into relationship with you and your business. To start with, you'll need a manifesto that clearly states what you stand for and how you want to make a difference to people's lives. This visionary statement will then breathe in deeply and stand tall when you successfully communicate it face-to-face with your customers in venue, online, at events and out in the wider world. And, I believe, when you encourage your whole team and your wider network to play a bigger part in building deeper levels of engagement with your customers , it will carry your business to a place that's simply head and shoulders above the rest.

One of the key concepts you'll come across in this book is the idea of 'Tribe-Building'. I believe it is a powerful new marketing strategy that will lead your business to truly stand out from the crowd. Many businesses try to market themselves to the widest audience. More savvy ventures will market to a target customer group, for example twenty-something professionals, families or affluent older couples. However, taking things one step further, I believe the smartest businesses will learn how to attract, engage and build long term relationships with their Tribe. The idea of the Tribe has come to prominence through books such as *Tribes*, written by one of the world's leading marketing gurus Seth Godin. Your tribe is made up of customers, employees and friends of the business who have become complete fans of your brand. As well as coming to visit you regularly, they will rave about your business to their wider network of friends and family. They will create awareness about your business and even physically drag people in the door who might never have given you a second glance before. Tribe members have quite a distinctive mindset. They are more likely to try new things and they will more openly appreciate innovation or high quality service. They are more likely to want to connect and be social, both in person and online. I suggest you pay great attention to this small group of customers as they are the group who can ultimately make or break your business. To start with, I'll describe the workings of a tribe in more detail and throughout the rest of the book I'll explain how to write a Tribe-Building Marketing Plan and how you can go about building and engaging with your tribe day-to-day, both online and in the face-to-face world.

As we progress, I will give you an overview of the latest marketing opportunities provided by the biggest social media channels such as Facebook and Twitter. You will also get an introduction to social media newcomers such as Instagram, Google+ Local and Pinterest who I believe are destined to play a much bigger part in hospitality marketing in the near future. I'll introduce you to the latest powerful online marketing tools that will transform your humble PC or Mac into a turbo-charged marketing machine, even on the smallest shoe string budget. And finally, I'll share my top project management tips for getting real, sustainable results from your team and your marketing activities.

The Story Behind the Book

Since the late 1990s I have worked as a digital marketing consultant with some of the world's biggest brands in technology, entertainment and real estate. By 2010, I had risen to a point where I was standing on stage at the Fast Growth Business Awards, staring out at the great and the good of British business. That night, in the absence of my inspirational CEO Karen Paterson (founder of Patersons Global HR & Payroll), I made a speech at the Fast Growth Business of the Year Award on her behalf and felt like I had reached the pinnacle of my career to date.

However, within just a few months it was all dramatically changed. Karen was replaced overnight by a new CEO. The company's American investors decided to slash the marketing team to a member of one, as we had done too good a job it seems! In the new CEO's words, the business brand was now boxing well above its weight. He explained the company was growing too fast and they needed to put the brakes on marketing until the rest of the business had stabilised and they could then continue on the road to ultimate global domination.

So exit stage left, my role as Head of Global Online Marketing at a fast growth technology firm, and enter stage right my new role as head chef and bottle washer of my very own digital marketing consultancy, The Loop Digital Communications. In May the following year, I got my first taste of working in the Hospitality sector when I started working with Tony McKinlay, a serial restaurant entrepreneur who had recently launched Platform Bar & Restaurant near London Bridge station. Tony and I had both been winning participants in the Southwark Tycoon Bootcamp competition run by the London South Bank University's London Knowledge and Innovation Centre. As a result of our win, we found ourselves sharing free office space in the University buildings at the beginning of 2011. When we first talked about working together, Tony had recently hired Jo Kruczynska as his new PA and Marketing Assistant. Jo was packed full of passion and enthusiasm for food and drink and she was already successfully blogging about her cake baking and supper club events at www.afternoontease.co.uk. However, Jo had never worked in marketing at any of her previous positions. Tony was keen to harness her knowledge and enthusiasm, but he also realised that she needed some guidance and training. A few conversations later, and we agreed that I would provide some strategic marketing advice to Tony and Jo alongside process, social media and marketing technology training for Jo. Little did I realise it at the time, but this was to set me on a course that would provide an exciting new focus for my marketing consultancy.

Around that time it was also becoming clear to me that we were sitting on the edge of a brand new era for marketing. I could see that expensive marketing agencies or large in-house corporate marketing teams no longer had an exclusive monopoly on delivering sophisticated, effective marketing strategies across the Internet. There was the potential for small businesses to do far more with their marketing budget than they ever dared previously imagine. This was a trend that I really wanted to help introduce to the world of small and growing businesses.

Despite my great enthusiasm for new technologies, I also remained cautioned by the knowledge that fault line cracks have a habit of springing up when you try to introduce new ways of doing things. Fear of technology is a big issue. Or perhaps it would be more correct to say that there is a fear of looking like a fool when trying to work with new technology. This fear can form a big mental block for many people. This scenario is compounded by the fact that new technologies seem to come flying around the corner every two minutes. It's a situation that is too often exploited by unscrupulous web development and marketing agencies. An uneducated customer is the perfect stooge to prey on when you want to make a fast buck and charge extortionate rates for a simple piece of marketing. For example, I could see many instances where marketing agencies were managing the design and delivery of email newsletters on behalf of their clients. However, despite the growing availability of cheaper online email marketing solutions, these agencies were continuing to use out-dated methods of delivery and they were failing to supply crucial results data that would help a customer to see the true outcome of their investment.

This was a route I was determined not to go down. I wanted to wake up in the morning and feel like I was delivering real value for my clients rather than just lining my own pockets on the back of their own ignorance. I figured I would deliver much more value long term if I focused on offering education and training alongside marketing consultancy and delivery support. As the old saying goes, sell a man a fish and he'll still go hungry tomorrow. Teach him how to fish and he'll feed his family for a lifetime.

Great marketing strategies, especially those that rely heavily on technology, are still prone to failure if they are not backed by sound project management. Over twenty years working in the digital marketing and media production industry has provided me with the perfect environment to fine tune my project management knowledge. Over those years I've been fortunate enough to learn from some fantastic project managers including Sharon Bambaji, a Prince 2 specialist, and Adam Gilmore, who's now a project management super guru at Microsoft. Both Sharon and Adam were colleagues from my days working at the children's book publisher Dorling Kindersley in the mid 1990s. Over the years, they have both generously shared with me the latest thinking in project management, through Facebook and online forums and again whilst I had the pleasure of working with Sharon in more recent times. On their recommendations, I took the time to further investigate and learn about these new management methods, and I subsequently pulled out many ideas that were successfully applied to later projects and other sectors.

Investing in my personal development has always been one of my top priorities. By learning to understand what makes me tick as a person and what situations push my buttons, I've slowly learned to take control of my unconscious impulses and become more confident in my own abilities. As part of this work I've examined how limiting beliefs or fixed mind sets could stifle not just individuals but whole businesses. I started to see that this one factor, more than any other, could make the difference between phenomenal success and desperate failure.

Over time, it's also become clear that the way I relate to my team members, and the behavioural boundaries I set for any team I manage, has another crucial part to play in the success of each new marketing endeavour. It was a point of great pride, when I discovered that there were more requests from employees to be relocated to my team than to any other team when I worked as Global Head of Online Marketing at Patersons Global Payroll. From day one, I had worked hard to support the development of a successful, productive and happy team. For me, that meant setting clear responsibilities and personal targets and fostering a safe place where all team members could voice their opinion and receive non-judgemental feedback.

Through my personal development work, I learned the importance of setting a personal vision and goals before setting out on any new phase. This activity is equally important and applicable to businesses, when owners and senior managers first start to define their company brand promise and brand values. It's not what we do, but the meaning that we apply to what we do, that also leads to great success or failure in life and in business.

Combining all these perspectives with the skills I've developed over the last twenty years has led me to step into the role I have now invented for myself as business advisor, marketing consultant, trainer and mentor. When I first discussed working with Tony and Jo at Towercrest, I had what you might call a light bulb moment. What I saw in front of me was the ideal client and the perfect industry that would happily combine my skills and experiences to one new, unique roll. This is a role that also allows me to share my love of good food, my personal passion for growing fruit and vegetables in my little urban garden and for sourcing local, seasonal produce.

Blackberries, plums, potatoes and tomatoes from our little urban garden

And so it has come to pass. Over the past two years since we first met, I have stepped into a role that has brought me amazing new levels of job satisfaction. I thank Tony sincerely for giving me the opportunity to work with him, his lovely wife Sarita and his amazing teams in London and Birmingham. At first, I only had a part to play in developing the marketing procedures at Platform in London Bridge, but over time I became more involved with the whole organisation and also had a chance to provide input on the marketing of Tony's oldest existing business, the Selly Sausage Café in Selly Oaks, Birmingham. More recently, I've been delighted to have a part to play in the launch of Le Truc, Towercrest's brand new bistro and bar which sits in the theatre and Chinese district of city centre Birmingham. On the back of my experience of working with Tony and his team, I've become committed to working as a specialist marketing consultant, trainer and coach in the hospitality sector.

In this book, I want to share with you the lessons we've learnt over the past few years that ended up with Le Truc successfully launching in Birmingham and Platform's bar and restaurant exceeding its targets by 10% in a year that has also seen bars and restaurants shut down in unprecedented numbers across the UK. Whether you want to learn how to do all your marketing in-house or you want to learn how to create a more educated brief for a freelance marketer, marketing or digital agency, this book will help you get much more from your marketing efforts, whether they are delivered in-house or not.

Overall, this book aims to do three things;

1. Introduce you to the concept of tribe-building and explain how you can integrate it as a strategy into your business marketing plan

2. Give you an overview of the latest channels, tools and tactics that can be utilised in venue, online and at events as part of your tribe-building strategy

3. Explain how you can deliver more successful results by involving your team and your wider network and by applying the latest approaches to project and people management

If you are looking for a get-rich-quick manual, I suggest you put this book back on the shelf right now. To my mind, no real victory can be expected in days or weeks. However, if you are committed to building your business for the long term, my mission is to offer you a plate load of food for thought and the inspiration to plan and deliver a marketing strategy that will bring you enduring success over the coming years.

CHAPTER 1

From Striving to Thriving

'It was the best of times, it was the worst of times'

Charles Dickens

Whatever side of the track you've found yourself on in recent years, it's been an era of extraordinary change for the hospitality industry in the UK. At the tough end of the scale, a whole series of issues have beset our local drinking establishments with pubs now closing at an alarming rate of 18 pubs per week within the past year[1]. This situation has been fuelled by higher alcohol taxes, the extortionately high rents and cask prices charged to tenant landlords by the big pub operators and the economic downturn more generally. In the wake of this tidal wave of closures, we've also seen the upsurge of a new type of drinking venue with over 425 new free-of-tie pubs opening since December 2008, along with more managed pubs and small family brewer pubs coming into the market place[2]. Many of these establishments have made their mark by offering greater beer choice, lower prices and a better environment for their customers.

Food has taken centre stage on the menus of many big pub operators and independents alike with 30% of turnover now reported as coming from food in a third of all pubs along with a 14% improvement in profitability for businesses who have taken this course[3]. However, the shift to offering more food will present on-going challenges in the coming years. A recent survey of UK restaurateurs had 57% listing rising food prices as their biggest concern[4]. It's not hard to see why when you hear that food inflation has surged from 3.3% to 4.5% in recent times[5] with some predicting a rise back to the previous 2008 inflation rate of 8% in coming years. Restaurants also have to contend with the fact that the total of food sales in the UK made by licenced pubs is twice the size of the licenced restaurant sector and this trend looks set to grow. Many restaurateurs are now thinking, 'if you can't beat them, join them', and are looking for ways to increase alcohol sales to their customers with cafés taking late licences and restaurants offering cocktails or a greater range of beers and ales on tap. We're also seeing a merging and mingling of food, drink and leisure that is resulting in brand new formats that combine food, drink and sports such as ping pong.

The more focused casual eating chains such as Giraffe, Pizza Express and Nando's are experiencing strong sales growth despite the economic squeeze. On the other hand, hospitality businesses who have not invested in branding and marketing and who have not found innovative ways to deliver value for money are scaling back venues or leaving the market place entirely. Additionally, the massive interest in fine dining, generated by TV shows such as the BBC's *Master Chef*, is taking the appetite for modern cuisine out to a wider customer base. The smart money is currently betting on up-and-coming chefs taking over as patrons at previously faltering country pubs and suburban drinking houses to offer a distinctive food and drink offer for people who are prepared to pay that bit extra for a quality food and drink experience in more relaxed surroundings.

I believe all this upheaval and change has created the space for the development of a better, smarter hospitality sector. Many failing businesses have left the industry, but they have been replaced by a raft of smart new entrepreneurs and talented chefs who are keen to find better ways to serve the modern customer. Other wily hospitality business owners and managers are still hanging in there after surviving recent tough times. Whatever category you place yourself in, I believe you have picked up this book because you are now looking for a smarter ways to make your business a big success. As a hospitality professional, you'll have a good idea of what constitutes good value and service. However, you also know that if a strong marketing strategy is not at the core of your business, all your other efforts will be in vain.

So I'm assuming we are both agreed that marketing is important. However, why is it that the hospitality sector often isn't prepared to make the investment in this essential business-building activity?

Symptoms of Minimal Marketing Investment

Sad but true. For a long time, the hospitality sector has been seen as the poor relative to many marketing professionals. As a rule, if you're looking for a well-paying career in marketing you'll hotfoot it to the finance, technology or consumer product markets. Only the biggest of the big casual dining and fast food brands have made significant investment into advertising, marketing and PR in order to get customers to the door and returning in their droves. Across the rest of the industry, restaurants, bars and cafés have heavily invested in the one strategy that was supposed to be a guarantee of success – by that I mean 'The Location, Location, Location Strategy'. Find a location that has great footfall in your local town or city centre, or make a beeline for a venue that is surrounded by the rich and the great. The only problem with this strategy is that it can be expensive, and in this day and age, it's becoming incredibly expensive if you want the best spots. Only last week, I read a tweet from a local bar owner in London Bridge who was incredulous to the fact that he'd just been offered a lease on a 2,000 square foot central London location for a whopping annual cost of £600,000. This might be quite an extreme example, but it's fair to say that the trend for ever increasing rents is not going to go away any time soon.

Then, there's the argument that the hospitality trade is a 'word-of-mouth' business. There may be some truth in this belief, but if you're launching a business from scratch, you will have no word of mouth coverage on day one. No coverage means no customers and in time, a big business failure if you're not careful. According to a National

Restaurant Association report (USA) the average restaurant marketing budget is 3% of total revenue[6]. On either side of the scale, that number can be more like 6% for fast growth brands and it's a sad fact of life that most underperforming hospitality businesses will invest less than 1% of turnover on promoting their business.

So what happens when a restaurant, café or bar does its best to 'save money' and invest as little as possible on marketing? Here are a number of typical behaviours that will result from this mindset:

1. There will be little or no investment in long term planning, marketing strategy development or brand development. Most marketing tactics will tend to be short-term and will fall into the category of local adverts or fliers, calendar driven promotions, discounts and two-for-one offers.

2. Customer information will not be collected, or if it is collected it will probably be stuck in a spreadsheet with no customer categorisation data and no output reports.

3. There will be little or no conversation with customers beyond the walls of the venue.

4. Marketing initiatives will not change much over the years. Perhaps the design and the wording will look different, but for all intents and purposes, it's the same promotion dressed up in new clothes.

5. There will be no proper investment in marketing technology. Owners and senior managers will settle with delegating marketing technology or social media marketing decisions to more junior and inexpensive staff. The thinking being, 'She's a young person, so she'll automatically know how to work this stuff for us.'

If your current marketing approach is packed with the above ingredients, I'm afraid to say that you are missing some big business development opportunities. A lack of investment in smart marketing ultimately means a lack of business, and that's a scenario I want to help you avoid at all costs.

Unsuccessful Marketing Budget Guzzlers

Of course, there are also those more well-heeled entrepreneurs who suffer from a big fat dose of 'more money than sense'. In these instances, marketing budgets can be squandered needlessly despite the best of intentions.

Today's unsuccessful money guzzling marketing tactics include:

1. **Print Advertising** – once a well-designed advert positioned in a prominent place in a local paper was one of the most successful ways to attract new customers or returning customers. However, cut to 2013 and newspapers readership is dying out at an alarmingly fast rate. Most young people no longer read any national or local papers and are far more likely to get their news from social media channels such as Facebook and Twitter. Then it's also worth mentioning print advertising's not so little brother, online advertising. At first, online banner ads were seen as the salvation of advertisers on the web. But, over the years, online banners and skyscrapers have become one of the lowest performing advertising assets you can invest in. There are a few exceptions. The beautifully sleek, video-based ads created by some of the country's leading agencies always do well. However, as soon as you cut out the inventive creative and the big traffic website position, most banner ads fail to perform and I'd suggest should be avoided at all costs unless you really want to burn a rather big hole in your budget.

2. **Fancy, Animated Websites** – I lose the will to live sometimes when I see a 360 degree panorama animation installed on the homepage of a restaurant website. I dread to think how many ordinary customers have website browsers that cannot view these movies and who may be put off exploring more about the venue because they had a technology malfunction. There was a big fashion in the past for highly animated websites, but these days the smart money is on providing a simple web experience

that gives the customer all the information they need in a well-laid-out, easy-to-access format. Many more people are accessing your information by mobile phone internet browser these days, so it's more important than ever to have a website that works well across all types of devices. Did you know for example, that iPhones and iPads can't playback Flash-based animations or videos? This situation can be rectified by programming animations with HTML-5 but lots of businesses have still not picked up on this fact and fixed the problem.

3. **Copy-cat Syndrome** – an owner or entrepreneur will see a new tactic working well for a competitor business or even another sector business, and without taking the time to work out if it's right for their business, they will demand that it is implemented forthwith. This can end up being a steep learning curve for more junior staff, with hours, days or even weeks of valuable time being wasted if this strategy is not thought through and implemented properly. Sometimes in fact, it will just not be worth the effort.

4. **The Big Launch** – in this case, the owner ploughs a lot of money into a big event which they hope will turnaround the fortunes of the restaurant in a single day. Dancing girls, flowing champagne and lots of freebies will be rolled out in an effort to bribe new customers to return at a later date.   Hey what's not to like about a great party? Only the bill and the lack of customer returns that follow.

5. **A Swanky PR Agency** – I've got absolutely nothing against talented PRs who work hard to do a great job for their clients. Unfortunately, the gun is very much loaded against a PR getting the sort of results that were once much easier to achieve. We now live in a world which is absolutely saturated with media. Everyone is exposed to thousands of new advertising and promotional messages each day via the Internet, mobile, street advertising, TV and more. Journalists can sometimes receive over a thousand new press release emails each day. Gone are the days when you could wine and dine a reporter or reviewer

in exchange for a more favourable review. It's an extreme sport sheer-face challenge trying to get anyone to pay attention to your message these days and honest PRs will tell you as much. Even when you manage to get an ace review, it's still no guarantee that you will last the course. Just last year, for example, the highly praised Galoupet in Knightsbridge closed its doors despite rave reviews from Zoe Williams in *The Daily Telegraph* and Fay Maschler in *London's Evening Standard.*

It doesn't matter how much money you try to throw at the old solutions. It's time to face facts and accept that the way to market your business has fundamentally changed. Today, all the old rules of marketing have been completely turned on their head. Smart businesses realise that they can no longer just push out press releases or promotional offers and then magic up incredibly loyal, engaged customers in the process. After over 150 years of push marketing, where he or she who shouts loudest wins, the clever money is returning to invest in the good old fashioned principles of relationship building. This shift has been enabled and reignited by the arrival of social media and other online channels which help businesses to engage more with their customers. Smart businesses are also focusing on the latest innovations and customer trends to ensure that they remain ahead of the game, delighting regulars and new visitors at every turn.

Rising Trends in Food & Drink Hospitality

In an age where most people are yoked to their computer screens and office chair each day, people are now seeking out opportunities where they can join together with others for a fun, cool or unique social experience. Across the board, your customers are now looking for eating or drinking out experiences that reflect their lifestyle choices.

The Little Guy Goes Big

Increasing numbers of people are turning their back on the chain restaurant or bar experience and are looking for a community-based, ethical or distinctive experience. Did you know that there are now approximately one thousand independent breweries in the UK? That's one for every 50 pubs and the highest number for over 70 years. The rise in popularity of craft beers has been supported by the new breed of local pubs who want to cater for the customer's growing knowledge of and affection for beers, ales and stouts that have character and great taste. These independent brews also spark the interest of the drinker with imaginative names that hint at interesting, locally-based back stories.

Other customers are responding enthusiastically to eating-out or drinking-out experiences that reflect their values and ethics. For example, innovative UK casual dining chains such as Zizzi are partnering with small, independent food and artisan designers and are telling stories about the people who create unique products on their behalf. Only this week, I ate out at a Zizzi restaurant in Central St Giles in London and I read in their menu about Kitty Travers *of* La Grotta Ices, the independent ice-cream and gelato queen who now produces a range of products exclusively for their dessert menu. On another page, I was drawn to a story about the graphic designer who had drawn a brand new typeface font for their latest menu and promotion posters. And on their twitter feed, I flicked through photos of stylish plates with fashion graphics that had been designed by another independent, up-and-coming designer.

All of these points of communication were drawing me into an engaging story about the restaurant. I no longer thought of the food and décor as an anonymous, corporate creation. Now I was starting to envisage a group of bright young people who wanted to engage me through their unique, creative offerings. I felt like I was supporting several young businesses. In fact, I ended up feeling much better about myself, knowing that my money was going to support the sort of businesses that could help dig Britain out of a recession economy. Think how much more powerful that idea is, than simply offering me a 50% discount off my main course.

More Provenance Please

The latest statistics on customer buying patterns indicate that pizzas, burgers and fish & chips remain the top preferences for most customers. However, these old favourites are being presented in fresh new ways, with information on the locality and name checks for the suppliers of the ingredients also included on the menu. A slab of locally-produced cheddar now has a starring role in your main course. The sustainably-sourced credentials of your battered haddock or cod are added to reassure the conservation-minded eater. For example, this flyer from Yo! Sushi fills the customer in on the sustainable and locally-sourced credentials of their fish.

Continuing in this vein, Jamie Oliver's recently opened Union Jack British Pizzeria concept offers wood-fired flat bread pizzas topped with distinctively British ingredients such as Westcombe Cheddar or Sparkenhoe Red Leicester which are lavishly described throughout the menu.

Themed Eating & Drinking

In the last few years, we've started to see diners and drinkers flocking to new activity-themed venues that combine games with food and drink. For example, All Star Lanes founded back in 2006, has rolled out four highly successful food, drink and bowling venues in central and east London and is now expanding in Manchester. The bowling venue's co-founder, Adam Breeden has also just launched Bounce, a 12,500 square foot 'social ping pong club' combining seventeen table tennis tables with cocktails and high-end dining. Think this concept is a one-off? I think we are starting to see a strong new trend here as in August 2012, in London's Earl's Court, we also saw the launch of Ping, a kitchen, bar and ping pong room venue with the capacity for 420, including 80 restaurant covers, two bars and three professional ping pong tables.

Healthy Eating

Healthy eating is a trend that is on the up and up with several chains now offering menus that either count the calories or offer healthier or gluten-free options in the place of carb- and fat-rich dishes. Zizzi and Pizza Express have both made an impact with figure-conscious diners by offering a selection of low-calorie pizza and salad options on their menu. Ping Pong, the Dim Sum and Cocktails chain, has healthy eating and low-calorie dim sum set options which have both proved very popular with their female clientele. Did you know that a customer who's looking to avoid gluten will often lead the decision as to what restaurant to eat at?[7] This means that even though customers looking for gluten-free options may only amount to one in one hundred, if you count in their spouses, friends or family members you could be missing out on a much bigger lost sales opportunity when you don't offer meals that cater to this group.

Talking about Food & Drink on Social Media

In the space where eating out and social media meet, we're seeing a large growing wave of social-savvy customers photographing and posting comments about their meals and drinks on Twitter, Instagram, Facebook and Pinterest. This new activity is offering up the perfect opportunity for restaurants and bars to interact with their customers through thank you messages, comments and chatty banter. Recently, I've read about Comodo, an enterprising Mexican restaurant in New York, which has added an Instagram hashtag and a message on their menu inviting their customers to upload pictures of their meals to Instagram along with this hashtag. As a result, customers can now search for the Comodo hashtag on their mobile before they eat and view photos taken by other customers who have eaten in the restaurant recently. These photos may not be the sleek, well-lit images that we're previously used to seeing, but they offer authenticity as a 'real deal' representation of the food and drink on offer.

Social media platforms such as Instagram are also providing a place where businesses can share visual stories with their customers and fans. Story-telling is an incredibly powerful marketing medium that is being used to fantastic effect by the top players in the business. Jamie Oliver is particularly brilliant at this. Every day he shares fun and vivid photographs on Instagram that give his followers a close-up view of his business and his life more generally.

These activities are just the tip of the iceberg when it comes to social media and I'll be talking more about how you can use these channels for marketing in Chapter 7 – Which Social Media Channels?

Foodies Bloggers

Food and drink bloggers have taken the scene by storm in recent years. It seems that along with fashion, food is one of the hot topics in blogger land. The most popular blogs will be followed by tens or even hundreds of thousands of followers, and each new rave review has the potential to send a gaggle of enthusiastic foodies to the lucky venue. I recently spent time researching the latest movers and shakers on the food blogging scene in London and I was amazed to discover that approximately one third of people who are describing themselves as a 'blogger based in London' were mostly talking about food and/or drink. Granted, some do a much better job than others. Eatlikeagirl, HungryinLondon and This Little Lady Went to London are just a few blogging food superstars who really stand out. TLLWTL claims to have 750 K viewers per month (verifiable by her host) and she covers not just food, but fashion, art, design, culture and more.

Many of the online review websites such as Urbanspoon are also scoring bloggers and connecting their regular blog content to individual restaurant, bar or café listings.

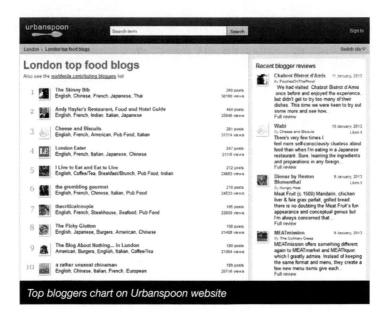

Top bloggers chart on Urbanspoon website

Overall the huge interest for talking about food and drink is opening many more marketing doors for hospitality businesses. You can read more about Food and Lifestyle bloggers in Chapter 4.

Online Feedback

More and more, customers want to know that they are being listened to. Where there is negative customer feedback on social media there is also an opportunity to sensitively handle the situation and create a better long-term outcome. No one likes to be ignored, especially if they are upset. Smart businesses realise this and are doing everything they can to respond to their customers' feedback on social media and review websites. For very little investment, it's now possible to put systems in place to make sure that you can monitor and quickly react to what's been said about your food, drink and customer service every day.

++++++

Many of the above new trends are throwing a serious spanner in the works for fans of the big fat hype. With mountains of genuine customer feedback oozing out from every corner of the Internet, it's next to impossible to sustain interest in your brand with hype alone.   The customer has basically got your card marked and won't be hoodwinked into believing your glossy spin on things. So forget the big launch, the glossy website and the silver-bullet 5-star national newspaper review. That strategy can only be pulled off by the finest of fine dining establishments at the moment, and I suspect that won't even be the case for much longer.

For everyone else, I would now like to reveal the ultimate formula for success. If you are to make your mark and keep customers coming back time after time, then I believe you'll need to build a tribe of highly engaged fans around your business. A tribe you say? What's that when it's at home? If you're ready to find out, then get ready to read on and I will explain.

CHAPTER 2

Kick-start your Tribe

What is a Tribe?

So, what exactly do I mean by a tribe? Let me roll you back to 2008, when Seth Godin, one of the world's leading thinkers on marketing, published *Tribes*, a small book with some very big ideas that describe the way the marketplace had changed. Godin has a fantastic knack for naming and describing new trends. In *Tribes*, he described a world where we are no longer satisfied with just working for a paycheque each month. Today we want to work on stuff we believe in. When we make things happen we feel much better about ourselves. We are less interested in buying factory produced goods or off-the-shelf ideas. Instead, we want to spend time and money on fashion, on stories, on things that matter or things that we believe in.

Looking back at the latest hospitality trends I described in the previous chapter, you can see Godin's view playing out in reality. We're seeing a huge trend in support for sustainable and ethical producers. Fun, stylish and innovative new formats are making a big impact with customers. Smaller independent breweries and restaurant owners are gaining ground over the big pub and dining corporates. Social media fans are avidly following the text and visual stories shared by innovative businesses and big personalities on Instagram, Facebook and Twitter.

Hugh Fearnley-Whittingstall is one fantastic working example of this trend. He is widely known in the UK as a bestselling cookbook author, TV chef and leading advocate for seasonal, ethically produced food. Since the late 90s he has built up the River Cottage business to encompass two canteens and delis in Axminster and Plymouth's Royal William Yard, which are supplied by a collection of local and organic food and drink producers from the South West. The business also delivers courses and special events that are inspired by the River Cottage ethos, ranging from dining and entertainment evenings, through to courses in foraging, curing, gardening, bread making, butchery and more. Fernley-Whittingstall's campaign for food sustainability has led in turn to the sustainability of his own business which is supported by his ever-growing tribe of engaged followers and customers.

The Rise of the New Market Influencers

Some of us now admire the new and the stylish more than we respect the long-established. Godin also describes a market place that has become led by the opinions of these trend-focused, early adopters who are the first to buy and the first to talk about new things. These new market influencers are not interested in average or big, flashy or expensive. What they are interested in is making connections and being on the edge of any new change. They also exhibit a powerful desire to contribute to and take from a group of like-minded people.

Your tribe must attract the attention of these new marketing influencers. If you can engage them as tribe members, they will rave about your business to a much wider audience. Tribe members aren't just customers, they may also be other business people who share and understand what you are passionate about. They may be suppliers, neighbouring business owners, managers and teams, consultants or other experts in your niche. Your employees are also top candidates to become some of your most vocal and loyal tribe members. When your business values involvement with its community, you also create an opportunity for community figures and members of public organisations to become part of your tribe.

In the past, people most likely heard about new things from their friends in face-to-face conversations. But now with the arrival of social media channels such as Facebook and Twitter, word-of-mouth marketing has exploded into a whole new realm. With the help of tribe members who are active online, your business now has the opportunity to go far beyond the boundaries of your local area, reaching out nationally and even internationally. This group of people create a fantastic new opportunity for you. Most organisations limit themselves by marketing to the crowd. I believe smart businesses set about forming a tribe.

The Essential Elements of a Tribe

According to Godin, in order for your tribe to take shape, some essential elements need to be in place.

A Clear Vision – firstly, your tribe needs a vision. Write a manifesto for your movement, make it clear what you stand for and what makes you different. Make your business an advocate for something that matters to you.

Be passionate – a vision without passion and belief will fall on deaf ears, so make sure your passion is on show.

Tribes need leaders – If there is no leadership, there will be no real commitment to the cause. Every good tribe needs a leader or a group of leaders to show the way.

Open the lines of communication – it's essential to make it easy for your followers to connect with you in venue and online.

Create connections – it's also important to enable tribe members to connect with each other. The desire to contribute and take from like-minded individuals is an essential attribute of any tribe.

Track and talk about your progress – Tribe members want to share your journey as you build the business. Celebrate your successes and share your progress regularly.

Please bear in mind, it's not about the money for your tribe members. Tribe members want to be part of something they believe in, that has meaning. They want services or products that reflect something about their personal preferences or lifestyle.

Once you've decided to assemble a tribe around your business, I believe this strategy will become the guiding light for all your activities hereafter. Are you ready to take the next steps? Then read on to find out how to kick start your tribe into action.

Your 5-Step Tribe-building Plan

Now you're ready to kick-start your tribe, let's look at each key step in turn.

Tribe-building step #1 – Write your Manifesto

According to the modern corporate branding manual, every successful brand must now have a vision, a leading statement that defines where the business wants to go. Visions are all well and good and hopefully will inspire us to reach out for some lofty, well-meaning goals.

When I think about a manifesto on the other hand, I immediately start to feel a fire growing in my belly. I can see a tall, wiry Russian guy, battling the atrocious weather. He grapples his way up unto the wooden stage and with a booming, determined voice, he addresses the small crowd in front of him. He doesn't care that the crowd is small and shivering. He firmly believes that he has got something to say that will set their minds and hearts alight. If he can deliver his message with clarity, relevance and passion, then there is a chance that each man and woman standing before him will set off with his message and spread the news like wildfire across the town.

Whatever you want to do, whether you want to pen a straight-up brand vision or put all your passion into a chest-beating manifesto statement, make sure it's one of the first things you do. Please don't get side-lined by tackling other marketing activities first. Put the website on hold and cool your boots on the social media until you've worked out exactly what it is you want to communicate about your business to the wider world. It doesn't have to be an essay. The best brand vision or manifesto will sit on one page, making it much easier to read and far more likely to be understood and delivered.

For example, here is a manifesto I found for The Soul Kitchen Community Restaurant. It may be a charity based business, but I believe it offers a fantastic example for food and drink service businesses across the board.

OUR MANIFESTO

All are welcome at our table.
At the JBJ Soul Kitchen, a place is ready for you if you are hungry, or if you hunger to make a difference in your community. For we believe that a healthy meal can feed the soul.

Happy are the hands that feed.
Those who volunteer are guided by Soul Kitchen staff through their tasks. Volunteering at Soul Kitchen can lead to qualifying for job training.

When there is love, there is plenty.
As you will see, our menu has no prices. You select what you like and make the minimum donation. If you can afford to donate more you are helping to feed your neighbor. If you are unable to donate, an hour of volunteering pays for your meal.

Good company whets the appetite.
At Soul Kitchen, neighbors from across the street or across town, new friends, families, those in need of help and those with help to offer, come together and share a good meal and the warmth of good company.

Friendship is our daily special.
Introduce yourself to the person seated beside you or across the table. Stay awhile and stay informed of all the ways Soul Kitchen is dedicated to eliminating hunger, building relationships, and celebrating community.

End the meal with a slice of happiness.
At Soul Kitchen the main ingredient is Love, with a large helping of you. Our chefs prepare our healthy, delicious meals with the freshest ingredients, some grown in our own organic garden. At the JBJ Soul Kitchen all are treated with cheerfulness, kindness, and respect.

Manifesto from the JBJ Soul Kitchen - www.jbjsoulkitchen.org

Techniques for Kick-starting your Manifesto

If you feel challenged at the thought of writing a vision or manifesto statement, these following techniques can help you get up and running.

1. Get It All Out On Paper

It may not be clear to you straight way what you want to put in your manifesto. You may have lots of ideas rolling around in your head but you can't quite put them in order. If this is the case, I suggest you get yourself a blank piece of paper and allow yourself to just write anything that comes to mind for the next twenty minutes. Don't worry about spelling or sentence structure. Simply write everything down and see what comes out.

If you are developing your manifesto with your business colleagues, get your team together and spend some time brain storming around a large piece of blank paper or you can write up your collective notes on a large flip chart. Allow everyone to have their say, and make sure to begin the session by setting your ground rules. To start, make it clear that every idea is free to be aired. Every idea is worth an airing. Participants should take turns in speaking and not speak over each other's input. If several members in the group are reticent to speak at first, it can help to get everyone to do the exercise individually and then get each person to read out their suggestions to the group.

2. Speak to your Ideal Customer

If you don't have a clear vision of your ideal customer at this point, it's really helpful to develop a handful of ideal customer personas in advance. Each persona will read like a short story. It will include details about their age and gender, what they like to do and what kind of person they are. It will also include other brands they like to follow and what issues they might want a solution to.   Once you've gathered this information, it will provide you with much deeper levels of insight into how best to attract your potential customers. To find out more about writing a Customer Persona, go to page 58 where I explain the process in more detail.

3. Be Affirmative

The words you use are really important. Affirmative language will make a far more positive impact as it implies your dedication to the desired final results. If you find yourself starting a sentence with 'We want…', scrub it out and replace it with 'We believe… ', 'We are…' or 'We will…'. If you want to experience the difference between these statements, I suggest you take a moment to close your eyes, imagine some positive outcome you want and then say, 'I want xxxx' to yourself quietly. How does that statement make you feel? Then repeat the exercise again, but this time imagine a positive outcome you want to deliver and then say to yourself, 'I will xxx'. How does that feel? When you start to feel the difference, I believe you'll become conscious of the support a simple affirmative statement can provide you with. Now imagine delivering a 'We want XXX' as opposed to 'We will xxx' or 'We believe xxx' statement to a much wider group. Which statement inspires you the most? Which statement do you think will inspire others to follow your lead?

4. Feedback

If you are working on your own, make sure to share your ideas with up to seven other people, so you can road-test your manifesto before bringing it to a wider audience. If you work as a group, get feedback from the team to see what values have the most support.

Tribe-building step #2 – Take the Lead

Every tribe needs a leader. Whether that's you or the leadership is shared with a group of people around you, your tribe will quickly run out of puff if the leadership issue is not taken seriously. There are plenty of people out there who call themselves leaders. Business directors, counsellors, preachers and community organisers may all lay claim to the title, but that doesn't necessarily make them bona fide, dyed-in-the-wool leaders. For a leader to honestly proclaim that title, he or she will need to exhibit three important attributes.

A Visionary Outlook – in order to write that all-important manifesto or vision statement, you'll need to be the sort of person who is always mentally jumping ahead into the future, looking for the next big opportunity. A visionary will make connects between new developments and old or new problems and will realise that one plus one could equal much more than two. Tribe members are always seeking out the new, so this visionary outlook is absolutely essential. Visionary leaders in the hospitality industry such as Alan Yau who brought us Wagamama, Busaba Eathai and Hakkasan, have that uncanny knack of reading or even shaping future trends and creating successful businesses that have sustained for the long term. For example, I can remember when Wagamama first opened in the 1990s and it had people queuing out on to the street to eat at its

Great Russell Street venue.   It appeared so futuristic at the time, with waiters taking our orders on their wireless handsets.   It really set the tone for the fast casual dining revolution that has spread right across the globe.

A Standard Bearer – for a leader to be inspirational, he will be a living, breathing example of the values and standards that are promoted by the business.   For example, there is nothing worse than a leader spouting off proclamations about investing in his team whilst behind the scenes he is sacking people on the spot and failing to deal with recurring staff issues. Tribes want to see their leaders walking their talk and in this age of increased transparency, woe betide the leader who thinks they can get away with perpetually doing one thing and saying another.

A Smart Decision Maker – smart and effective decision making is what makes the best leaders stand out from the crowd. Delayed decisions can often result in lost opportunities and blocks to growth. I recently worked with Donal Carroll, an author and business thinker who's been a leading contributor on the Open University's 'Creativity, Innovation and Change' MBA module.   At his recent book launch event, he referred to a photograph on his Facebook page that shows a man jumping across a crack in the road that had been created by an earthquake tremor. When the earthquake first hits, the crack is quite small and it's easy enough to jump over, but if the business man hesitates for too long, it won't be long before another tremor widens the crack into a much more daunting gap. And so it goes with decision making.   Take too much time making your next move and it gets more and more difficult to move on. Tribes thrive on forward momentum so slow decision making could seriously hamper your tribe's growth.

What if you're reluctant to become a leader? What if you're worried that you won't match up to the task in hand? It's important to realise that true leadership skills don't just appear overnight.   For most of us, these skills are slowly acquired over the years through trial and error. The best thing is to aim for a good enough starting position and then throw yourself into the experience. You'll be amazed how many personal resources you have to call on when you start to get on with things.

Take inspiration from famous leaders. If you find yourself drawn to a particular leader, seek out his or her biography and read about their lives, challenges and successes. Recall their stories during times of adversity to help give you another perspective on what to do next. Steve Jobs' biography written by Walter Isaacson is a particularly popular read in this regard, as is *Losing My Virginity* by British business tycoon Richard Branson.

If you're new to a leadership role or you feel you could do with some added support, a business coach or mentor can make a huge difference to your personal performance. It's a coach's job to ask you powerful, leading questions that will help you reflect on your issues. Once you have identified and named the issues that are blocking your success, you are then much better able to visualise smarter solutions to your current predicaments. Sometimes you'll have to learn how to deal with external factors that are not in your immediate influence. If you are stuck because you are holding on to a limiting belief, a coach will help you to examine the root causes of this belief. Through this process you can diminish the hold this belief has over you and you can learn how to make decisions without being influenced by unconscious impulses.

Tribe-building step #3 – Open the Lines of Communication

Once you've got the vision and leadership wheels in motion, you're now ready to consider how to open up the lines of communication with your tribe. Tribe members naturally like to talk, react and comment. They want to tell you if they've had a great time and they want to share that news with everyone else. They love it when you recognise them and address them by their first name. When considering what channels of communication to use, it's a good idea to go back to the customer personas you previously developed to support the development of your vision. It would be lovely to be able to suggest that you use just one channel for communication with your customers, but in our current hyper-connected, multi-channel world, it's essential to take the time to work out which channels are going to suit your customers best. Are your tribe members hooked on social media, or are they from an older generation who value old fashioned face-to-face interactions above everything else?

If you want to get your tribe's reaction to your latest specials menu, you could invite your special customers to a tasting preview event. These types of events give you a perfect opportunity to ask for feedback and to collect insights into why your tribe members keep coming back. On-line surveys can also be setup very cost effectively these days using online services such as www.surveymonkey.com or www.google.com/intl/en_uk/enterprise/apps/business/. You can invite customers to give you feedback in exchange for a tasting event invitation, or a complementary starter or cocktail when they next pay you a visit.

When I started to work for Towercrest, we decided to get some customer feedback on the venue layout, service, pricing and perception of value. Rather than simply run an online survey, we wanted to make sure that we captured the opinions of customers who visited the bar and restaurant at different times of the day and week, so we could be more confident that we had collected the widest range of opinions. It didn't take long to write a questionnaire and set it up online using a free Google Docs form. Our reservations assistant used an iPad to call up the questionnaire in venue and then she methodically selected customers at different points of the day and week, and offered a complimentary drink to the customer in exchange for a few minutes of their time to answer some questions. The resulting feedback was incredibly useful and helped us to make a number of changes from a more informed perspective.

Social media channels also provide many excellent ways to engage in a regular two- way conversation with your customers, partners and the wider community. For example, just a couple of minutes ago, I received a tweet from the Dishoom Bombay Café in Covent Garden where I ate out last night. Someone from their team has picked up on the fact that I tweeted a favourable review and photo of their spiced Skate Cheeks tapas dish. (It really was delicious by the way!) Co-incidentally, I decided to order that dish last night as I had seen someone else rave about it on Twitter earlier in the week. As soon as I first tweeted the message, I also received a tweet back from London Buzz, a twitter service that collates and scores positive review mentioned on twitter for London restaurants, bars and other visitor destinations.   I was immediately able to see how well Dishoom scored with other tweeters and I could see if my thoughts were shared by other people. For me this is a fantastic example of a restaurant that is simultaneously making an effort to thank me and connect me to the wider tribe of their twitter fans.

Even though I'm a massive fan of social media communications, I'd suggest you don't throw the baby out with the bathwater by forgetting that non-Internet savvy people can also have a thirst for new things. I know plenty of people who like to explore a city, town or country area by foot. My sister for one has travelled to every single continent on the globe through her job as a cabin crew supervisor for Gulf Air. She loves to explore each new city she visits yet she will rarely turn to the Internet for recommendations on new places to visit. You may decide to speak directly to curious passers-by such as my sister with a humorous or eye catching welcome message on a street easel blackboard.   These messages shouldn't be confused with straight-up advertising. Instead you can aim to amuse or intrigue with a statement or message that reflects your brand personality. Here's a rather surreal example from my client Le Truc, in Birmingham. I don't know about you, but this would definitely stop me in my tracks and put a smile on my face! A funny little statement like this can act as a conversation starter once people arrive in your venue. It has the potential to have a much more magical effect than a standard promotional 'two for the price of one' message. By implication, you are saying, 'we are friendly, come in, visit us and have a chat'. You are also addressing one of our most basic human delights when you encourage us to raise a smile and connect on a less transactional level.

'A Board' message from Le Truc – raising a smile with local passers-by

Tribe-building step #4 – Create Connections

When people are in tribe mode, they don't just want a two way conversation with the leaders. Tribe members love nothing more than to share their passion with other like-minded souls. For example, in cities all over the world, foodie tweeters like to meet up at TweetUps where they can meet face to face to swap stories, contacts and ideas. There's a real buzz about meeting others who will happily share your obsession for seeking out the perfect flat white coffee or who will happily accompany you around a food fair to find the tastiest gourmet burger on offer.

As tribe leader, it's your job to help your members connect with each other in as many interesting ways as possible. An event can be a great way to get everyone together. You might celebrate your business birthday with a special charity raising event or musical evening. Always make an effort to give your event a unique twist, so it gives your tribe members something new to talk about. If you want to support a charity, try to find one that resonates with your values. If you're a city restaurant that makes a point of offering local, seasonal produce and you value being an active member of your local community, you could decide to raise money at your birthday event for a city gardening charity. For example, there are a growing number of charities in the UK who seek to rehabilitate ex-offenders or people with mental health issues by teaching them gardening skills. If they sell their produce on the open market, you could also take your relationship another step forward and use the charity as a local supplier for some of your fruit or veg.

At first, this sort of strategy might seem like more effort than it's worth, but over time this type of activity can translate into the development of a much more meaningful relationship between you and your customers. I had the pleasure of interviewing Shaun Alpine Crabtree recently, who is the manager and part-owner of The Table Café (@thetablecafe) on Southwark Street in south London. A few years ago he met up with the organisers of Putting Down Roots, an initiative run by St Mungo's charity for the homeless which helps to rehabilitate the homeless through gardening. At the time, any unclaimed fruit and veg ended up on the compost heap. Shaun quickly jumped on an opportunity to stop this food waste by offering to buy produce from the gardens as it became available. Shaun's initiative is a brilliant example of creating connections with a community group which in turn leads to a deeper values-based connection with his customers. For more about St Mungo's visit : http://www.mungos.org/pdr.

Partnering with like-minded businesses on events can also be a great way to attract new members into your tribe. If you can discover a common subject of interest with your partner, you open the door to all sorts of engaging new ventures. For example, Le Truc, my French restaurant client in Birmingham, has recently developed a joint venture with the Electric Cinema, the city's historic and much loved independent film house. The restaurant is only a short walk from the cinema. The businesses realised they had common ground as they both cater to people who have a passion for all things French. On the back of this realisation, they decided to club together to organise a French cinema and food evening. The cinema arranged a screening of the French arthouse favourite, *Amelie*. Before the show, Le Truc provided the starter course and special cocktails for the attendees and later the guests walked around the corner to the restaurant for their main course and dessert at Le Truc. The event quickly became over-subscribed and the partners ended up running a reprieve of the offer the following month.

Social channels also provide a brilliant space for your tribe members to spot and interact with each other. Make sure to use your social media channels to individually thank and interact with the customers, partner and supplier businesses, media professionals and local organisations that form part of your tribe on Facebook, Twitter et al. This activity encourages the development of new connections between your tribe members as you give them greater visibility. At first you might wonder how an activity like this will affect your bottom line. If this is the case, bear with me a moment while I draw you a little analogy. Imagine that you are the host of a fantastic party. All the great and good of the town have shown up and you're the one person in the room who knows everyone else. As the night progresses, you play the part of the host with most. At every turn you see another opportunity to introduce another good friend to a new contact. By the end of the evening, everyone is shaking your hand as they leave, telling you what a good time they had and how it was great to meet so many interesting new people. Perhaps even a few bright new business liaisons have sprung up as a result of these impromptu meetings. What sort of impression do you think you'll have left everyone with? Will they look forward to coming to another party soon? But more importantly, how do you think they might speak about you to other friends and colleagues after the event?

Every time you help your tribe members to connect with each other, whether it's in person or online, you're making a small but important investment into your long-term social and business worth.

Tribe-building step #5 – Track & Talk about your Progress

As the old adage goes, it's the journey not the destination that matters. Your tribe wants to go on a journey with you and have the inside track on what happens next. As your business builds, take the time to celebrate and share your little successes. When we're really engaged and want to sing your name from the rooftops, your successes become our joy, so we love to hear it whenever you have good news to share. For example, as I write, Amanjot Johl, the bar manager at Le Truc has just won a national cocktail-making competition which is a really big deal for all the team. At the time of writing, the bar and bistro has only been open for three months so it's wonderful to be able to share such good news and see the great feedback it's started to generate on Le Truc's Twitter and Facebook walls.

With the latest Timeline feature on Facebook business pages, it's now also possible to add posts that celebrate important achievements from your business past. This facility gives you an opportunity to share your journey over time and allows tribe members to dive deeper into your back story. The bravest tribe leaders share the journey warts and all. If you want to hear a fantastic 'no-holds barred' story from one of the world's highest profile restaurant entrepreneurs, then I highly recommend you read Danny Meyer's *Setting The Table*. In his best-selling book, Meyer is amazingly generous with his insights, and he's equally frank about the factors that led to his successes and failures.

++++++

Now you have a road map for kick-starting your tribe, it's time to focus on the marketing plan that will make sure your tribe goes from strength to strength.

CHAPTER 3

Your Marketing Plan

The purpose of the last chapter was to get you to think about the perfect conditions for growing your tribe. We're now going to look at the more practical task of integrating your tribe-building strategy within your marketing plan and its delivery. Before settling down to writing the Marketing Plan proper for the coming year, I recommend you take some time out to review your existing marketing activities. This is especially relevant if you've been in business for at least a year or more. If you're a start-up business you can jump over the following and jump straight to the Situation Analysis section on page 53.

Where are you now?

As an existing business, it's likely that you'll already have plenty of marketing collateral to work with. You'll have a brand logo and perhaps a strapline. Like most hospitality businesses, you're likely to have a website, in venue flyers, posters, menu boards, menus and external menu displays. If you've a forward-thinking small café, bar or restaurant or a larger chain business, you'll have a computer based customer relationship management system in place, a loyalty card scheme, email marketing and various social media accounts. And then you'll have a record of all your online listings and local advertising spots. To start with, I understand that you will not be able to wave a magic wand and instantly call up the funds to make sweeping changes to all your marketing collateral. This is why I'd like to introduce you to the audit. A marketing audit will give you a steer on what marketing actions are important and what actions need to be prioritised in your marketing plan. It will help you to set benchmarks on your existing marketing performance. It's also a process that will help you to identify early, quick wins.

The first step is to list everything you currently do as an output of your existing marketing plan. Any statistics or analytics you have gathered from the previous year's marketing activities are reviewed and summarised in order to give you a benchmark for your existing level of success. What was your total turnover for the previous year? What percentage was your Gross Profit and your Operating Profit (before Tax)? How much did you spend on marketing in the previous year and what percentage was this spend of your total turnover? Collect the data from your existing social media accounts. (For more on gathering social media analytics read page 171) Do your best to collect all of these figures. Once in place, they will help you to move into a much more powerful business position. Information is power, as they say. If you have a clear view of the numbers generated by your business activities, you're creating a situation where you can get a better overview and in turn, make better, faster decisions.

In the second part of the audit, you will include recommendations on what you need to stop, start, do more and do less of. Every activity needs to be viewed through the lens of the tribe strategy. What initiatives or tactics do you think will make the biggest impact on growing your tribe? I believe a marketing audit is one of those jobs that is best carried out by a marketing consultant. You could have a go at doing it yourself in-house, but a fresh pair of experienced eyes can see things that you might have missed due to your close proximity to the business. A consultant can also include your management team in the process by running a workshop to review and assess your marketing activities and performance statistics to date. Bringing more people's experience into the mix is likely to give you deeper, more valuable insights into what works, what needs to change and what new initiatives need to be added to the mix.

Creating your New Tribe-building Marketing Plan

Once your marketing audit is complete you're ready to start work on your new Marketing Plan. At a minimum every Marketing Plan should include these essential components.

Situation Analysis

Every good marketing plan will include an analysis of the market, your local competition and a SWOT analysis (your business' top five Strengths, Weaknesses, Opportunities and Threats). For your market analysis, do your research and find out what are the latest innovations in your niche. What do the big research companies or industry magazines herald as the next new trends in your business sector? Describe the market segment you are looking to attract. Are your principal target market young, hip customers in their 20s or 30–40 year old professionals? Then think about the market needs. What are your customers looking for? Are they seeking an intimate, comfortable space? Or are they looking for a bright, high energy place where they can entertain and socialise with friends? Is there an opportunity to provide a service to groups or corporates? Look at the competition. Is anyone else providing a similar offer? What do they do well, and what could be improved on? What are your competitors charging for similar dishes or drinks? You can take some of the top line results from your audit and feed them into your SWOT analysis. Listing your top five strengths, weaknesses, opportunities and threats in order of importance will sharpen your thinking further about what you need to prioritise. If you do need to make big changes this will become more evident once your audit and situation analysis is complete.

Brand Assets

Brand development is a core part of any marketing strategy. When you develop your brand it should include some core statements that clearly state what your brand represents. These statements or assets include:

- Positioning Statement

- Value Proposition

- Core Values / Beliefs

- Mission Statement

- Brand Promise

Here's your step-by-step guide to defining each of your brand assets in more detail:

1. **What's your Positioning Statement?**

   What sort of business are you? How do you differ from other businesses? Are you a pop-up or a friendly, family business? Do you offer accessible cuisine or hearty, home cooked favourites. Are you a gastro pub or a Francophile-style wine bar and café? Find the perfect words to describe your business. Consider how those words will resonate with the lifestyle choices of your desired tribe members. Are you a tea lounge or a tea room? The former denotes a hipper, modern take on drinking tea, whilst the latter conjures up a picture of old ladies, lace and chintz. With a few more carefully chosen words you could indicate whether your tea room was a nostalgic reconstruction for the cupcake loving twenty somethings or a charming, old world hideaway for local ladies-who-lunch.

2. **How do you Provide Value or Benefit to the Customer?**

   When you answer this question, it's best not to think about the products or services you provide. Instead, think about the value you create or the benefits you offer that will appeal to your customers. Are there lifestyle references or preferences that your potential customers can hook onto? For inspiration, here are a few colourful descriptions I recently read about two of Dublin's favourite city bars in a local city centre guide.

   McDaids in Harry Street, Dublin was described as '... a very cosy, shoulder-to-shoulder affair where an unbeatable

Guinness is only a quick shuffle away and commenting on overheard banter is de rigueur. The perfect place for whiling a night away righting the world's wrongs with a few close friends or over a quite pint in Brendan Behan's memory.' In other words, it's small and often packed, and the vocal volume increases steadily as the night progresses, but the way it's described makes a feature rather than a negative of what's on offer. This description is sure to appeal to customers who are looking for a popular, sociable drinking venue.

In contrast, Hogan's, another very fine drinking establishment on Dublin's South Great Georges Street, was described as a more spacious, relaxed alternative. 'Hogans could easily be located somewhere in the East Village of Manhattan but to say that would be an injustice to its typically Dublin crowd. The large windows look out onto flower sellers and cycle chic passers-by whilst inside remains the home to the laid back people watchers, good time seekers and newspaper readers.' This description lets you know that this is a pub where you can have a conversation without screaming over your pint. As a feature, this is sure to have its fans too.

3. What are your Core Values and Beliefs?

Identify the top seven values that underline your business. For example, do you care about using sustainable ingredients? Or what do you think are the important characteristics of your team? Write your beliefs, motives and intentions about each value. For example, if you have 'Respect' as a value, you might say the following: 'Without mutual respect, we believe it's impossible to deliver the awesome level of customer experience we want to be remembered for. Regardless of how difficult things may get, everyone in our team will always show respect to their colleagues and our customers'.

Here's a nice and simple example of a Values Statement from the D&D restaurants group who own a number of well-known restaurants in London including Quaglinos, Skylon, Butlers Wharf

Chop House, Floridita and the Bluebird restaurant in Chelsea. They state:

Our Values

Achieving 'sustainability' across our 20 London restaurants may seem a lofty goal, but we realised a while ago that it's all about looking at what we're doing in a new light.

Sustainability

We believe that if you're not doing something right, change it, so across the business we have taken action, from joining the Sustainable Restaurant Association (SRA) back in 2009 to buying more energy efficient ovens. Transparency is important and by Christmas 2011 all 20 of the D&D London restaurants will have been assessed and achieved a sustainability rating from the SRA.

Good food

Good food is integral to our business and we have longstanding relationships with many of our suppliers. Exceptional animal welfare is a priority, as are certain criteria such as food that is GM-free, natural and as British as we can reasonably ensure. We have also signed up to the Sustainable Fish City campaign run by Sustain, which aims to get London businesses adopting a sustainable fish policy by the 2012 Olympic and Paralympic Games.

Pride in what we do

Like our people, each of D&D's global restaurants is very individual, and chefs have the freedom and flexibility to seek out unique, seasonal produce. A sense of pride and ownership is positively encouraged in each of our businesses and, as such, we run a number of industry-renowned training programmes to promote staff development.

4. What Is your Mission Statement?

This statement will be a single sentence that spells out why you are in business. Your mission statement is for your internal use only and is something you'll share with employees, investors and partners in the future. Once you've outlined your values, it will be much easier to write this statement as it will feed on the work that you've already done up to this point. For example, here are a few mission statement examples from some of our biggest food service names:

Pizza Hut: 'We take pride in making a perfect pizza and providing courteous and helpful service on time, all the time. Every customer says, "I'll be back!"'
McDonalds: 'McDonald's vision is to be the world's best quick service restaurant experience. Being the best means providing outstanding quality, service, cleanliness, and value, so that we make every customer in every restaurant smile.'
Jamie Oliver's Better Food Foundation: 'Our mission is to educate and empower as many people as possible to love and enjoy good food.'

A great mission statement should lay out your ambitions as a business and help set a benchmark for how you want to do business.

5. What are you Promising the Customer?

Your brand promise is a public promise that will guide your employees to provide the most awesome version of your desired customer experience. I particularly like this extract which I found on the The English Restaurant's website blog.

'We aspire to be friendly, relaxed and efficient. Our culture is one of civility, decency and moderation. We are proud of our sense of belonging in our community – and connect with this at many points. We are a family-owned, independent business, but still somewhat in our infancy as a restaurant. It may be that sometimes we fall short of the high standards we set ourselves, but we hope we are making steady progress in the right direction.'

For the full statement visit: http://theenglishrestaurant.blogspot.co.uk/2012/10/mission-statement-lines-written-on.html

Customer Personas

In my previous life as a corporate website producer, I was introduced to the idea of writing a selection of customer personas at the start of each new web development project. These personas or fictional stories came out of some initial customer research. Each customer persona has a name, an age, a career, family life and education history that is fleshed out further still with a description of his or her learning style, attitudes, expectations, motivations and experience goals. Once complete, the persona descriptions were then circulated to everyone involved with the project. From this point on, these stories helped inform the decisions made about the website copy & design and the potential pathways created to respond to different types of customer behaviour.

I was delighted to find that one of my new restaurant clients was already working with customer personas as part of their overall marketing strategy. This has proved to be an incredibly helpful reference point when developing tactical marketing initiatives. For example, earlier this summer I was working with the restaurant's in-house marketing manager and we were brainstorming some ideas for a seasonal Facebook campaign. One of their key target customer groups is 20 something, female, aspirational and very sociable. She enjoys meeting up with her female friends after work and she likes to chat about life and love over a few swish cocktails. When it came to the World Cup, we struggled to think how we could put a spin on the event for our purposes. But as soon as we asked the question, 'what would Lucy do?' it all became very clear. Lucy will probably wave goodbye to her boyfriend for the next two weeks as he and his mates become completely engrossed in the soccer fest. It's likely that she'll plan plenty of 'girl-only' evenings to help her get away from the beer cans, pizza and football in the living room. In response, we devised a 'No Ball Games' series of posts that started with a photo of a 'No Ball Games' park sign and an invitation to flee the World Cup coverage and come to our 'No Ball Games Zone' at the restaurant. There 'Lucy' and her friends could join us for a 'Complimentary Cocktail' with meals eaten during match times throughout the World Cup. The campaign created a real buzz with very high levels of engagement. Later over the tournament, we posted reminder notes with photos of boyfriend types lounging on the sofa watching TV with beer and pizza, as a little reminder regarding our 'escape plan'!

With our tribe-building strategy in mind, it's a great idea to use this process to help you build up a vivid picture of your ideal customer. It's worth bearing in mind that she will have additional special attributes that won't be found in your normal customer. If you reel back to the earlier chapter when I first talked about the attributes of a tribe, you'll remember how tribe members are more likely to be advocates of the new, the trendy or the specialist niche. They will be more likely to seek out products and places that they find interesting. They are less likely to be creatures of habit who will settle for the same experience year in and year out. In this group, you're talking to people who are likely to be sociable and who may have travelled more than the average Jo or Jane. Think about these qualities and consider how they could be weaved into a persona description of your ideal tribe member.

Here are a few additional recommendations to keep in mind when you decide to develop some customer personas as part of your marketing plan.

1. Don't create too many personas. If you can keep it to three or four, it helps people within your business to recall the stories more readily. A persona that is easily remembered is more likely to be used.

2. Circulate your first draft personas to your team, and see if they ring true to your customer facing staff. If not, ask for feedback and see if they can be written with more authenticity.

3. Once written, refer to your personas frequently, especially when you are developing new marketing content.

4. Why not also use them as an inspiration for the kitchen and bar team's product development sessions?

Marketing Channels

Once you've got a good mental picture of your ideal tribe members and some examples of your more everyday customers, you're now at a point where you can research and select the most appropriate marketing channels for your business. I know this task can be one of the most confusing for business owners and marketing managers. Today, there is an incredibly diverse range of channels you could potentially use to market your restaurant, café or bar. The biggest problem for most small businesses is working out which channels are the best ones to use.

For now, I've listed the main marketing channels on offer to restaurant, café and bar businesses in the following chart as an aide- memoire. If you're confused about what channels will work best for you, I suggest you spend time reading Chapter 4, 5 and 7 which will give you a much better insight into how to best utilise these various channels for different types of businesses. As an initial pointer, I've highlighted some channels that I think will be particularly useful to you if you decide to apply a tribe-building marketing strategy.

Channel Category	Channels
Advertising & Direct Marketing	Tourist guide & directory adverts or listings
	Poster sites
	Magazine and newspaper adverts
	Cinema & TV advertising
	Mail Outs
Digital	**Email newsletters**
	Website
	Discount websites (Groupon, Social Living etc.)
	Reservation websites (TopTable etc.)
	Review websites (TripAdvisor etc.)
	Restaurant directory listing websites
	Search Engine Optimisation (SEO)
	Reciprocal website links
	Till receipt feedback
	Blogger adverts/sponsored promotions
Social Media Channels	**Facebook (Page, Apps and Adverts)**
	Twitter
	Google+ Local (Google Places)
	Instagram
	Pinterest
	FourSquare
	YouTube
Customer Relationship Management	Loyalty cards
	Digital vouchers

Channel Category	Channels
PR	Press and magazine editorial coverage
	Blogger reviews
	Radio and TV coverage
	Awards
In-House Print & Signage	Menus
	Posters
	Flyers
	Feedback cards
	Post cards
	Venue signage
	Blackboards
	Street A boards
Special Events	Pop-up restaurant events
	Food fairs
	Food or drink promotions at partner venues
	Tasting events
	Classes & demonstrations
	Pub crawl events
	Restaurant birthday celebrations
Sponsorship	Charity or event sponsorship
Publishing	Recipe book
Business Networking	Attending regular business networking events (BNI etc.)

The Essential Elements of a Tribe-building Channel

OK, so you're looking at all the above channels and you're wondering which ones are going to work best for you. If you're committed to attracting and developing a tribe around your business here are the main things to consider when picking marketing channels that will work best for your brand.

I recommend that you invest in channels that will help you to achieve the following:

- **Develop a Conversation with your Customers**
  Two-way conversation is life-blood for the development of your tribe. Online, social channels are the big winners in this regard. They provide infinite ways for you to interact with your customers, so they need to be a core activity in any tribe-building strategy.

  If you activate your business account on review websites such as TripAdvisor, you will also open up another opportunity to interact with your online customer reviewers. Once registered, you can respond to reviews and make much more impact with customers and potential tribe members by delivering a fantastic online customer response.

  Events of all kinds from pop-up restaurant nights to tastings and festival stalls also provide fantastic channels for getting direct face-to-face feedback from your customers.

- **Deliver Distinctive, Memorable or Innovative Experiences**
  According to Seth Godin, in his book *Purple Cow*, the only brands that stick out these day are the ones who concentrate on delivering innovative, delightful, out-of-box experiences that go on to remain indelibly etched on people's memories. For example, a creatively delivered, themed evening is a great way to make your restaurant stand-out. My restaurant client, Le Truc, recently hosted *Soirée Pompette* which was billed as a night of French cabaret featuring French cuisine, *fantastique* entertainment and *scandaleux comportment*! The whole evening was presented

in French to a mostly English-speaking audience, but it was handled very cleverly by the entertainers. Everyone seemed to get the gist and enjoy the humour. The piece-de-resistance was a session of French Bingo that had people leaning back and ear wigging across the tables to get a hint of what the numbers were in English. It proved to be a fantastic sell-out night with over 300 covers sold and definitely helped to favourably promote the restaurant within its first couple of months of business.

- **Enable your Tribe Members to Interact with Each Other**
Again, events and social media channels provide hundreds of ways for tribe members to interact with each other, strengthening the case further still for their inclusion in your strategy. For example, share success stories on social media from your food supplier enabling them to connect in interesting new ways with your wider community and your customers.

- **Tell a Story about your Brand**
One of the best ways to connect with people is through story-telling. These days, stories are more likely to be told through photographs, especially on social media channels such as Instagram. The tiled photo presentation on this site makes it really easy for viewers to make connections from one image to another. Think about the stories you want to tell that help to personalise your brand. What has your team been up to? Have you been working with anyone interesting? Are you researching something new? Did you go on a trip to find new ingredients? Did you celebrate a big occasion recently? Facebook photo albums are also a good medium for story telling when you want to reach a wider customer audience. You can also have prepared word-of-mouth stories that you can share with people when you run a festival stall, visit local networking events or when you host special in-venue gatherings.

- **Connect with your Customers' Wider Interests**
Partner with a theatre, a sports team or a charity in order to find ways to connect with your customers' wider interests. The end

result could be a social media promotion, a specially-themed event or fundraiser.   If you organise a cooking demonstration, you can also create a way to connect with your customers' interest in home entertaining, healthy eating or family cooking.

Avoid channels that:

- Have no interactive element whether that's digital or face-to-face

- Only allow you to shout about promotions

- Advertise your business to an unsuitable audience

Goals, Targets, Strategies and Tactics

To be in business, you need to be financially viable, so it's all important that you include goals and targets that keep you focused on improving your bottom line.   You will also need to outline the strategic moves that you will take to help you realise your vision. For example, you may have an overall marketing goal to generate an increase in your business turnover and a performance target to increase your turnover by 25%. In order to achieve this, you're going to implement a tribe-building strategy that will attract customers who become enthusiastic word-of-mouth ambassadors for your restaurant, café or bar business. Tactically, you plan to deliver this strategy by investing in a customer relationship management system, a new electronic loyalty card scheme, social media marketing and by developing special themed events with strategic partners.

Your plan should expand on each tactical activity in more detail, with an overview of the specific channels you will use, the campaign ideas or activities you will implement, and the milestones or important dates associated with each activity.   As well as revenue-building goals, you should consider performance-improvement goals such as increasing the amount of time you spend on marketing planning and marketing education with a view to improving your overall performance.   You can also set goals and targets for keeping track of your performance results, so you are better able to judge the success of your marketing investments.

I highly recommend you also set benchmarks and goals for your social media activity. Keep track of the number of followers and fans on each of your social media accounts. More importantly, track your engagement and influence ratings to gauge how well you are interacting with your online tribe. The influence rating provided by www.Klout.com is becoming one of the most well used indicators of social media success. You can read more about how Klout works in the Analytics section of this book. Facebook also keeps track of how many people have engaged with your page through post likes, comments and shares and displays this under your main Facebook banner image as a 'Talking About This' number. Using the Facebook Analytics panel you can track how many people you reached with your most popular posts. This 'Reach' number will include fans and friends of fans and indicates how many people saw the post in their newsfeed. Tools such as www.TweetReach.com also enable you to see how many people you have reached on Twitter over a period of time via mentions of your Twitter address or a hashtag you are promoting. Here's the Le Truc TweetReach report after an artists event they ran in venue not long after opening.

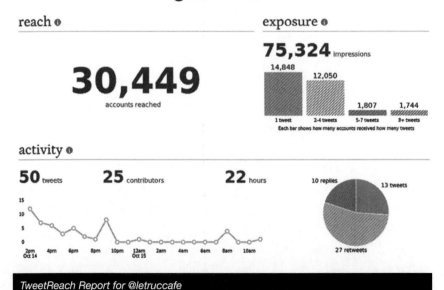

TweetReach Report for @letruccafe

At a minimum, I suggest you set milestone targets (e.g. 5,000 Twitter followers by end of 2013) and you track the numbers on the following metrics each month:

- Number of Followers or Fans for each account

- Number of New Followers or Fans for each account

- Facebook 'Talking About This' score

- Your Klout Score

- Reach of your most successful Facebook post or Twitter hashtags

- Then review these numbers at least quarterly, to assess your progress and to make decisions for generating further improvements.

Sales Forecast

Set out your projected and actual sales figures for the coming year. Once you roll into the new financial year, make sure you keep track of your actual turnover and GP for food and drink sales. Dependent on the sophistication of your EPOS (Electronic Point of Sales) system, it will be very useful if you can also add weekly cover numbers and sales figures for your main lines whether they be breakfasts, lunches, dinners, sharing platters, bar food or particular drinks. This information will give you even better insight into what is working well sales wise and what needs additional marketing support.

Marketing Expenses Budget

Forecast your marketing expenditure for the coming year. What third party services will you invest in and when? Will you need to invest in marketing training on new technologies? Do you have an in-house designer or someone who can do basic artwork from templates? If not, how much will you budget to pay for design support each month? You'll also need to factor in web development or updating costs, menu development, flyer and poster printing and monthly fees for email marketing software, customer relationship management software and any of the other online solutions you decide to invest in. Again, set out columns for your projected and actual spend, so as the months go by you can make sure you stay within budget.

To get a more realistic idea of your budget you can use the following estimator charts to work out how much time and resource you should allow for marketing activities in the coming year and how much spend you should allocate to external marketing expenses. Typically, your budget will work much harder if you invest it at those points when you are usually busiest.   For example, don't waste big chunks of your budget trying to get more customers in the door during your quiet times between 3pm and 5pm. It's better to spend more at Christmas and other seasonal high points, especially if you are supporting these marketing campaigns with more expensive marketing activities such as specially designed menus and printed promotions. A much used marketing statistic reminds us that new customer acquisition is seven times more expensive than marketing to existing customers, so make sure you allocate ample portions of your budget to encourage repeat visits, increased spend and bigger parties.

Marketing Activity Time Estimator

	HOURS PER MONTH											
Marketing Management Activities	J	F	M	A	M	J	J	A	S	O	N	D
Marketing planning												
Briefing, team and planning meetings												
Research and skills development												
Customer database management												
Social media planning & management												
Review website account management (TripAdvisor etc.)												
Menu development												
Email newsletters – creation and delivery												
Door drop flyer campaigns												
Seasonal campaign development (Christmas, Valentine's Day etc.)												
In venue promotional graphics (Specification & artwork design)												
Monthly analytics and statistics reports												
Website updates (DIY or 3rd party management)												
Event organisation (food fairs, tastings, classes, pop-ups, street food events etc.)												
PR liaison, media pack creation and updates												
Promotional partner liaison												
Attending local business networking events												
Corporate liaison and marketing offer / pack creation												
Award entry co-ordination												
Monthly totals												
ANNUAL TOTAL HOURS												
ANNUAL TOTAL DAYS Divide by 6 to estimate total person days per year you need to allow for marketing activities*												

* I recommend you divide the hours by 6, as it's rare that you'll get a full day of productivity for particular tasks. It's always sensible to allow some contingency for on-going jobs such as reading emails, dealing with general enquiries etc. and time out during the day for comfort breaks etc.

External Marketing Costs Estimator

Marketing Activities	J	F	M	A	M	J	J	A	S	O	N	D	Annual Activity Total (£)
PR consultancy fees													
Marketing consultancy fees													
Web design and development fees													
Marketing training courses, books, magazines and other professional development resources													
Advertising													
Printing													
Photography													
Flyer and poster design													
Menu design													
Signage design and production													
Website updates													
Customer Relationship Management software subscription													
Social Media management software subscriptions													
Social Media analytic reports (If you're a larger business you'll be wise to invest in good reporting software)													
Email newsletter management software													
Online booking fees (include discount taken from sites like TopTable for taking your bookings online)													
External event registration fees													
Award entry fees													
PR Newswire distribution fees													
Local business networking fees													
MONTHLY SPEND (£)													
ANNUAL TOTAL BUDGET FOR 3RD PARTY COSTS (£)													

++++++

Now you've got the key elements of your marketing plan in place it's time to think about the day-to-day activities that will take your plan from vision to reality. In the following chapters, I will help you to focus on answering the following important questions.

1. How will I use the Internet to attract new tribe members?

2. How will I attract visiting customers to my tribe?

3. How will I turn my team members, business partners and the wider community into highly engaged tribe members?

CHAPTER 4

Connect With your Tribe on the Internet

Do you know what a Zero Moment of Truth is? This is a phrase coined recently by Jim Lecinski, Director of US Sales and Service at Google. He uses Zero Moment of Truth[8], or ZMOT for short, to describe a point in time when a customer moves from undecided to decided about a product or service. In the past, that moment was likely to occur when the prospective customer saw an old media 'Stimulus' such as an advert, a TV commercial or a press article. The other main place where a customer might make a buying decision was at the actual point-of-purchase, in the store, or in our case, at the door of the restaurant, bar or café. This point-of-purchase decision spot was previously named as the First Moment of Truth, or the FMOT, by the advertising gurus at Proctor & Gamble with the Second Moment of Truth occurring when the customer experienced the product or service and had a good or bad reaction.

So, what's so special about the Zero Moment of Truth? According to Lecinski, the ZMOT only happens online. More importantly, it is also judged by 84% of purchase decision-makers to be the point when they are most likely to make a buying decision. This statistic marks an incredible customer behaviour change from the pre-Internet era to now.

So what are the characteristics of a Zero Moment of Truth? Here's how Lecinski lays it out:

- A ZMOT might result from a web search on Google, Bing, Yahoo or YouTube.

- It can happen at any time of the day or night and is increasingly happening as a result of a search on a mobile device.

- The customer pulls what she wants from the web rather than being the passive recipient of a message that's been pushed to her.

- This decision is emotional. She is invested in finding a solution that she wants to satisfy.

- It's a conversation with many people involved from friends and family, connections on social channels, to other customers, experts, reviewers, bloggers and marketers.

Despite this customer behaviour becoming an established fact for a few years now, businesses are still not investing enough in online marketing. More than ever before, I believe it's essential for you to buck this trend and to get your business firmly involved in the online conversation that's running around your business.

To help you get to grips with the latest online opportunities, I'm now going to give you a whistle-stop tour of today's essential web-based marketing channels. As well as social media, we'll look at business websites, how to improve your ranking and visibility on search engines, email newsletters, food and lifestyle bloggers, online review websites and online discount services.

Using Social Media to Market Your Business

To start with here is my 10 step guide to setting up and using social media as an effective marketing channel for your business.

1. **Research your Customer's Use of Social Media**
   Firstly, you'll need to establish which social media channels are most used by your ideal tribe members and which channels are

most popular with your wider customer base. Tribe-minded customers often use a couple or even several channels as they are especially interested in being connected, but your wider customer base may be less social media savvy and stick to only one or two channels at most. The best way to do your research is to speak to your customers and ideally, do a short online survey (more of which in Chapter 8 on Your Essential Digital Marketing Tools). Ask which channels they use and which one they spend the most time on. Talk with your marketing manager or marketing consultant and members of your team who regularly use social media. Record how they answer this question and add it to your research.

2. Know what your Best Competitors are Doing on Social Media Channels

Notice I advise you watch only your best competitors. To be honest, there is not much to be gained by following the social media activities of all your competitors, especially if they are not using social media very well. That's a big waste of time as far as I'm concerned. The smart approach is to seek out competitors who are doing the best job. For example, fanalyzer.co.uk lists the top pubs and clubs and the top restaurants on Facebook in the UK. Take the opportunity to watch and learn. In some instances you'll want to model similar winning strategies for your business. On other occasions, you'll want find a way to stand apart from the market. Keep a sharp eye on the competition to make sure you successfully hold your point of difference.

A simple way to keep track on the competition is to create Facebook and Twitter lists. The Twitter lists feature is accessible via your Twitter Profile page. Just click on Lists on your Profile page (in far left column) and then click on the 'Create List' button near the top of the screen.

Lists Subscribed to / Member of	Create list
Hospitality Marketing by Susanne Currid 🔒 11 members	
Restaurants Cafes Bars by Susanne Currid 🔒 45 members	
My Favourite Charities by Susanne Currid 3 members	
Friends by Susanne Currid 🔒 28 members	

Lists View in Personal Profile view on Twitter.com

Once you've named your list you can add Twitter accounts to the list by clicking on the little menu that usually appears beside the Follow or Following button next to the name of the Twitter account. Click on the arrow to open the menu and select 'Add or remove from lists' to add the account. Then whenever you want to check out your competition on Twitter, just select Lists again then click on the list you want to view. This option gives you a chance to quickly scroll through your competition's tweets on a daily or weekly basis.

To keep an eye on what your competitors are doing on Facebook, you can use their 'Add Interests' option that appears at the bottom of the left hand column of your Facebook newsfeed page (the page you first see when you login to Facebook). Just click on 'Add Interests' then on the next screen click on 'Create List'. This brings you to a 'Create New List' popup screen where you can search for businesses by name in the Search field and then add them to a list you call 'Competitors'. Once your list is setup, there will be a link to the list under the Interests heading on the left hand column of your Facebook newsfeed page. These list setup options make it much easier to keep a track of your competitors for the future.

Creating a new List in Facebook

Adding Facebook page to an Interest List

3. Choose your Channels Wisely

If you're a very large hospitality organisation with at least a couple of dedicated marketing managers at your disposal, then perhaps you can rise to the challenge of managing a social media presence on every channel available. However, if your resources are more limited, stick to focusing on generating content for the top three or four channels that are proving popular with your tribe and wider customer base. If you spread yourself too thinly, it's likely that you'll never do anything particularly well. Each channel will need a customised approach. Even though social media publishing solutions now allows you to publish one message on several platforms at once, it's rarely the case that one type of message will suit every channel, every time. If you are a small business or start-up, the argument for focusing on two channels maximum is even stronger. Pareto's Law states that 80% of your results will most likely stem from 20% of your efforts. With research and an initial trial and error approach, identify what works best for you and then plough most of your resources into these channels.

4. Have a Customer Response Strategy

Whether your customers come to laugh, cry or scream on your social media newsfeeds, make sure you have considered how and when you will respond. In my opinion, every post from a customer should be responded to in the fastest time possible. Ideally, never allow more than a day to go by before you give a response. Thank everyone for their kind or complementary comments. Mention their name when you respond. It's said that our name is one of the sweetest sounds we ever hear and I'm certain that's just as much the case when we are mentioned online. It's wise to consider how you can keep an eye on your social media channels on shift or a rota basis, so you're there to respond to your customers from open of business to end of evening, seven days a week. This is especially important for bigger businesses who will generate a great deal of social media response.

Consider how you want to address your customer when they have an issue. I recommend you take the conversation to email as quickly as possible if they have a plausible sounding dispute or complaint. If an active complainer keeps coming back with a 'not good enough' response that may be an indication that they are pushing their luck for a goodwill freebie. Don't fall into the trap of giving more than you would normally do. If you know what your limits are in advance, you're better prepared to deal with these issues on the day. But what if the conversation gets nasty? In the case of trolls AKA people who get a kick out of being actively malicious on social media, the best policy is to take the conversation offline or onto email asap. Publicity is oxygen for people who behave in this way. If they are just not prepared to engage in any sort of civilised dialogue you also have the final option of silence, followed by putting a block on their account. In these instances, I've often seen other more loyal customers come to the brand's rescue. I think most people have the good sense to see when someone is being highly unreasonable. As long as you keep your cool, you'll be able to address these scenarios without serious comeback.

5. **Listen Proactively**

Do you know what customers are saying about you on social media? Whether you're a big chain or a small, neighbourhood business, your reputation in the market place is now being led by what ordinary customers are telling their friends and family about your brand. Did you know that social media allows people to mention you without necessarily talking directly to you via your social media accounts? In effect, thousands of public comments could be flying around without you ever knowing. The way to remedy this situation is to setup systems that allow you to instantly track, read through and respond to these conversations from one place. There are now plenty of tools on the market which allow you to keep an eye on and respond to this communication whether it's about your brand, a venue or a promotion you're offering. Check out the chapter on Marketing Tools for more about these tools.

6. **Integrate Social Media Activities with the Rest of your Marketing**

You're already probably getting the idea from reading this book that social media is not an activity that stands on its own. Smart businesses find ways to use social media communications to support other marketing and business activities such as events, in-venue promotions, recruitment, requests for feedback and more.

7. **Invest in Training and Resources**

Social media is skills and time-intensive, so if you decide to manage this part of your marketing in-house make sure you enable the person who leads your Social Marketing to either take time out to study the latest tactics and social media technologies, or invest in intensive training sessions with a social media expert to ensure they can stay up to speed without spending too much time away from the day-to-day management activities. Make sure your team are using best-of-breed social media management and analytic tools so they are not wasting time on repetitive tasks and they have immediate access to results reports.

Your front of house team also needs to know what's going on. It makes real sense to run regular Social Media strategy and technology briefing sessions so your customer service teams know what the latest plan is and how to support social media initiatives on the floor. It's also vitally important that business owners and leaders stress the importance of these briefings as that will make your social media marketing initiatives more likely to be taken seriously and acted upon. It's still too easy for the uneducated to dismiss social media as a waste of time.

Even with the right tools and training, you still need to allow time and resources to generate daily social media content and to keep up to date with your customer communication. If you're doing social media right, you'll spend a lot less on advertising and PR. It's a case of diverting your resources to the place where they will make most impact.

8. **Measure the Results**

There is nothing worse that aimlessly rolling out strategies without reviewing the results. Keep a track of your follower numbers. Record your engagement levels which will give you an even better indication of how well your content has been received. How many people re-Tweeted your special promotion on Twitter this month as opposed to last month? How many people viewed your photographs or special event coverage and shared it with their friends? How many people went to your website from Facebook or Twitter? How long did they stay on your site once they got there and what sections did they visit? Did you get the results you were looking for? If not, make amendments to your plans and review and compare the results a month later. Month-to-month this is going to be one of the best ways to see if you are gaining ground and mastering social media for your business.

9. **Have a Strategy for Keeping up with the Next Social Media Trends**

   Do you know what's coming next? Have you got a plan to stay on top of new trends? Business opportunities arise out of finding and capitalising on new trends and innovations, so make sure someone is keeping you abreast of the next new thing.

10. **Write a Social Media Marketing Plan**

    As the old saying goes, fail to plan and then you inevitably plan to fail. After doing your research and developing your responses to the previous nine points, funnel all this information into a social media marketing plan. Finally, condense this plan into a One Page Plan that's easy to pin up on the wall and circulate to your whole team. Even the best strategies are useless if they are rarely looked at after they've been written. A simple overview like this can become a highly powerful tool which helps keep your whole business on track.

Social Media Management: In-House vs Marketing Agency

You may wonder why I've placed so much emphasis on managing your marketing activities, and especially your social media, in-house. After working both client-side and in agencies for the past fifteen years, I've come to the conclusion that day-to-day marketing is managed much more effectively in-house. I think there is still a role for marketing agencies to play, but their specialism and value usually lies in providing advice on a new strategy direction, developing new branding and in providing new marketing collateral for international, national or large-scale marketing campaigns. Independent marketing consultants can also help bridge the gap when your in-house skills don't meet the mark and you need additional part-time support each month or on a seasonal basis.

I bring up this subject, as I believe social media is very much about day-to-day communication. To do it well, it requires a deep knowledge of your business and your specialisms. Marketers often work for a range of businesses and sectors, so they are not necessarily experts in your subject. They don't live and breathe your business in the way an employee might come to do. I sometimes describe the difference between working for an agency and working in-house for a client as being like the difference between two people who are just dating and two people who are married. This is especially the case when you're working in the hospitality industry. There are going to be plenty of times when you want your social communications to react to events that are taking place in the evening or over the weekend. If you've got an in-house person who's happy to work different types of shifts, who will attend events and tweet or post on your behalf whilst managing other aspects of the event as well, you just end up with a much better, more authentic form of communication. If you choose to farm this activity out to an agency or an off-site consultant to manage, I don't think it's ever going to be quite the same. It's likely to feel more hollow and corporate and provide no real insight of what's actually going on in your venue. Your marketing manager can also multi-task on other activities as, of course, you won't just need him or her for social media. With the right person, it's not just more effective, it's also a more cost-effective approach to making the most of your annual marketing budget each year.

Your Website

Despite all the recent clamour and excitement about social media, you still have to have a great website in place. This is one of the main places where your customer will research what you have to offer. In effect, it's your dedicated online showcase and information point. So what are the essentials you'll need to present on your site?

- Latest food and drinks menus

- Location details and map

- Booking information / Online Booking

- Social media links (e.g. Twitter and Facebook)

- Information for group bookings and/or corporate hires

- Seasonal or special events

- Press coverage & latest news

- Recruitment

- Contact form

In terms of how your website should work, these are my top tips:

Keep it Simple

My number one top tip – keep it simple. Make sure your website works well across all devices from pcs and macs to mobiles and laptops. Gone are the days when it was all the rage to have an animated introduction. Any sorts of animated gadgets or gizmos may not play back successfully on all the different browsing devices the world now has to offer. Don't frustrate your customer with unnecessary whizzy bits. Keep it simple and just supply the important information.

MeatLiquor's ultra simple website

Keep it Up-To-Date

There is nothing worse than seeing a year old menu on a restaurant website. It says with big flashing lights that your business is not on the ball. When you commission your website make sure it includes a content management system that allows your in-house team to update your menus and information pages on your latest events or news.

Take Online Bookings

If you take reservations, make sure that customers can make a table booking on your website. This is an easy enough option to add to your website when you use a website widget or code provided by one of the online reservation websites. Alternatively, you can have a developer create a bespoke online booking form. You may especially wish to do this for group Christmas bookings or larger event bookings.

Promote Your Social Media Content

Make sure to add links to your social media channels on your homepage or top navigation bar so people can see them regardless of which page they are on. Include a Twitter or Facebook feed on your website, so visitors can see what you and your customers are saying about your food, drink, service and events. This will keep your website fresh looking and will indicate that you are open to communicating with your customers. This of course is going to ring the right bells with your potential tribe members as they'll be immediately looking out for ways to interact with you when they visit your website.

Invest in Great Photography

Get the best photographer you can afford. The old saying goes that we eat with our eyes first. Whet your customer's appetite and thirst long before they arrive at your venue with fantastic images of your interiors and what's on offer on your menu. If you're promoting a more trendy vibe, you may not want to fill the site with food shots and instead you might concentrate more on creating a mood. The Meat Liquor website photography (previously shown) is a great example of this approach, with its dark alley and moody neon sign background shot. In an instant you get a smell of its edgy vibe.

Be Contactable

Include an online form so customers can contact you at any time of the day or night. If someone wants to make an enquiry about a booking at 2am give them the option to do that with an online form. Add an option for customers to sign up to your email newsletter. If they want to keep you in mind for the future, make it easy for them to do so.

Businesses such as Yo! Sushi who are especially hot on customer service serve us a fantastic example of a great Contact Us form. In the form screen grab you'll see they go the extra mile to ask the awkward questions. For example, what was your experience like? And how would you rate your experience? In the left hand column, they provide names contacts for the kitchen, marketing, health & hygiene. This speaks volumes about the levels of accessibility they provide. The contact form also uses tone cleverly to connect further still. The use of the smiley and unhappy emoticons helps the business to relate to the customer on a friend-to-friend level. All in all this is a fantastic example of great online customer communications. It's no wonder they win so many plaudits for service.

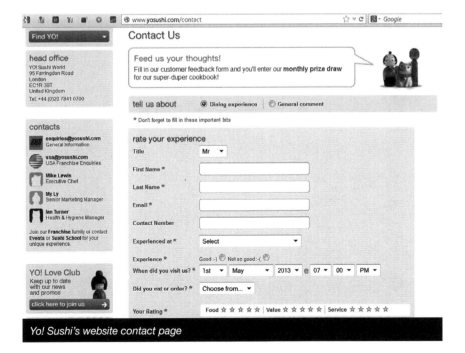

Yo! Sushi's website contact page

Search Engine Optimisation

If a customer decides to search for a venue like yours on the Internet, make sure you are as visible as possible on the big Internet search engines such as Google, Bing, Yahoo etc. Customers typically search for location, type and quality, for example, 'best Italian restaurants in London'. Make sure your meta data, the website code which describes what is included on your web page, includes details of your venue type, value offer and location. The major search engine optimisation gurus also suggest that you make regular references to these points as recurring key phrases in your website copy to increase your visibility further still. Another point that has a big impact on your listing position is how many external websites link back to your website. Make sure your site is listed in as many places as possible, and especially on those sites that get big audiences. It's also worth bearing in mind that the major review websites such as TripAdvisor are finely tuned to achieve the best listings in the top search engines. As a result, if a customer searches for your business by name, your website search result is most likely going to sit alongside the TripAdvisor review page search result for your venue. If your star rating on the review site is good, your TripAdvisor or other directory star rating is certainly going to encourage a customer to click directly on your website search result.

To illustrate what I'm talking about, below is an example of the Google search results for Le Truc, which shows the website results sitting alongside the restaurant's TripAdvisor listing. Notice the stars on the TripAdvisor result. I think that's a fantastic indicator of quality at the point of search and will help encourage customers to click through at this point.

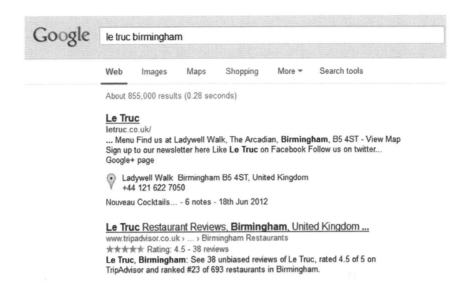

Search Engine Optimisation (SEO) is a very broad and fast-moving subject that needs more space and analysis than this book allows. For more detailed advice, I highly recommend you either keep up to date by checking on websites such as www.searchenginewatch.com or you speak to your local SEO consultant.

Email Newsletters

Email newsletters provide an excellent way for you to stay in touch with your tribe members and your wider customer base. It's true that your customer's inbox is often flooding with messages from competing quarters. However, when newsletters are smartly designed and cleverly integrated with other communications channels they can prove to be one of the best online marketing tools you have to hand.

Here are the main points to keep in mind when devising and sending email newsletters:

1. **Build your List Organically** – Do not be tempted to buy an email list from a database seller. OK, it might seem like such

a simple option. Just buy the list, send an email. What's to lose? Well firstly, most email newsletters sent out to cold lists have an appalling open rate. If the customer doesn't know you from Adam, why would they be even interested in opening your email when they've got so many others to get through from people or businesses they actually know? The best way to build your list is initially harder, but it will be well worth it in the long run. Simply invite your customers to sign up for your newsletter on your website, on your Facebook page and through special promotions in your venue. Your ultimate task is to find innovative and appealing ways to make this invitation. The average open rate for marketing emails is about 27% currently (Q3 2012 figures from Epsilon)[9]. But well marketed businesses can expect to achieve much higher open rates especially if they have nurtured their tribe of followers.

2. **Use Email Marketing Software** – Don't send the email from Microsoft Outlook, Gmail or whatever you use to send business emails. When it comes to bigger mailings it's much wiser to use Email Marketing Software solutions as: a) they will enable you to create an email that looks more attractive b) they will tell you how many people have opened your email and clicked on your links and c) these solutions will also enable customers to automatically unsubscribe from your list. This last point is important as it's required by law when you send out mass mailings. You also want to keep your customer data secure, so using a password controlled Email Management account will help you to stay on the right side of the law in this regard.

3. **Control your Email Frequency** – Don't send emails too often. I think the optimum frequency for a restaurant or bar is once a month. More often than that and you are more likely to be ignored and you could rack up more unsubscribes. If you have a specific campaign, perhaps you want to promote your Christmas dining offer, then you can increase the frequency to maybe once a week. But don't do this for more than a month and don't run higher frequency campaigns like this more than a couple of times

a year. Great content, occasionally served is the best recipe for success here. If your email content is strong, your customers will look forward to reading your monthly emails and will not feel like they are being bombarded.

Food and Lifestyle Bloggers

The food and lifestyle blogging phenomenon has gathered a huge head of steam in recent years. It seems people like to blog about food and drink more than practically any subject except fashion and beauty perhaps. Bloggers are always on the hunt for the next best thing. In fact, they display all the hallmarks of the tribe member mentality and are some of the biggest influencers around within their spheres. Switched-on hospitality businesses that focus on quality or the on-trend end of the market have taken to courting bloggers at special tasting events and demonstrations. Some of the most successful bloggers are also providing advertising space or sponsored promotional features for a fee.

As a group, they can be divided into two main groups for our purposes. On the one hand you have foodie bloggers who are all about the food or the drink. He will totally focus on what it tastes like, how it looks, how innovative it might be and its provenance. The foodie will also care deeply about the venue, the service and the ambiance. The foodie blogger will generally be looking for an angle and if he doesn't like what's been served, watch out! A scathing review will surely be the end result. A word to the wise. If you don't think your venue can hack this intense scrutiny, there is no point in courting the foodie blogger's attention.

On the other hand, you may want to consider connecting with lifestyle bloggers. Style and experience are far more important to this blogger. She won't line you up against the wall if your food doesn't get 5 stars. Instead, she's more interested in your venue from a social point of view. Is this somewhere my followers might like to try? Was there something unique or delightful about the venue? Generally these bloggers have wider appeal as they also talk about fashion, beauty, travel, or their home town experience. If you're aiming at a younger, more wired demographic it could be well worth while getting to know your local lifestyle influencer.

Your Blog

Alternatively, you can decide to run your own blog. Many blogs have already been set up by restaurants, bars and cafés and have been used to promote the stories behind the dishes and products on offer to their customers. Blogs also give you a channel to share photos of the team and your visitors, in effect to provide a more human face to your business.

I especially recommend a blogging strategy to hospitality leaders who have plenty to say about the customer experience, new trends and their personal experiences within the business. If you want to be a thought leader in your sector, someone who can show the way to others, a regular blog will provide you with a fantastic platform to speak directly to your audience and the wider media. A great example of leadership blogging is provided by Bill Marriott, the Executive Chairman of the Marriott International Hotel Group. Even at 80 years old, he still regularly shares his views and experiences of the hospitality business to his international online tribe. You can have a look for yourself at www. blogs.marriott.com.

Online Customer Reviews

Online reviews have become an increasingly powerful influencer when customers go to the Internet to research new eating out or drinking venues. And frustratingly for you the owner or manager, reviews are the one thing you have very limited control over. As a larger business you could be the recipient of waves of daily critique from the passionate blogger, the food fanatic or deeply disgruntled customer. If you're a smaller business, you may have fewer reviews and the misfortune of having that awful review you received a few months ago sitting in the full light of day for all to see.

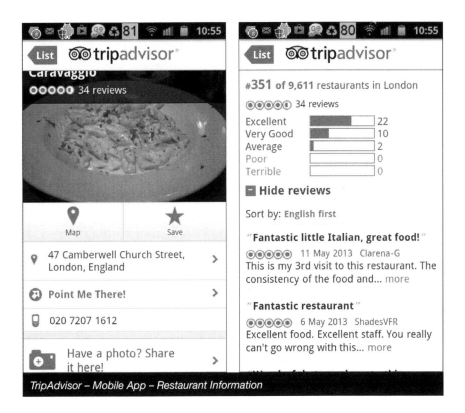

TripAdvisor – Mobile App – Restaurant Information

Whatever your size and whatever your thoughts about reviews and the sites that host these reviews, I believe they still offer you a huge opportunity to attract and engage with your tribe and wider customer base. In the UK, today's biggest dedicated review sites include TripAdvisor.com, the world's biggest travel site, Yelp.co.uk, Toptable.co.uk and Urbanspoon.com. As I write, it's rumoured that even Facebook wants to get into this space by allowing diners to review and rate restaurants from within the restaurant's business Facebook page.

Thankfully, the biggest sites now give owners an option to respond to customers. For example, as a business you can register an account on TripAdvisor, update your information and respond to reviews from customers. Yelp also has an 'add owner comment' link at the bottom of every customer review which gives you a chance to respond directly to any issues that crop up. Not all sites will give you this added control, but where they do, take advantage of the feature. Here are my top tips for responding to negative online reviews:

1. **Get Signed Up –** Is your business signed up on the review sites that matter in your area? If not, make sure you get registered asap, so you can start to interact if the option is available on the site.

2. **Make Someone Responsible –** To start with, delegate this task to someone in your business. Ideally, I would get a general manager or deputy manager to keep tabs on your reviews each week.

3. **Don't Respond in the Heat of the Moment –** I know how it feels when a customer leaves a bad review. Immediately, it starts to get your heart rate up and it's hard not to feel annoyed. When feelings are high, this is not the time to respond. Instead, step back, take some time out before you reply.

4. **Review –** If it's a serious issue take a day, in fact why not take a few days to consider what's been said and to see if you can see the issue being repeated in your venue? Ask other people in your team. Does this negative comment resonate with anyone? If so, consider how you can rectify the issue and make amends. If it really seems like a one-off it should be enough to thank the reviewer for their feedback, acknowledge the point made, explain what action you will take to avoid this happening again and invite the reviewer back to your venue to see how things have improved. If you can go the extra mile, invite the reviewer back and suggest they ask for you by name. This will give you an opportunity to talk through the issue and show how much you want to make amends. This proactive approach could potentially give you a much bigger win so it's well worth trying. If you end up with an extremely satisfied customer, why not ask her to revisit her review and leave a fresh comment. Never make it a demand. This needs to be delivered as a humble request. A turnaround review is one of the most valuable things you can seek to generate on the web, so it is always worth aiming for.

5. **What if the Reviewer Starts Ranting and Raving for No Good Reason? –** This type of situation can happen unfortunately.

When it does, don't give the argument any additional oxygen. Simply acknowledge the complaint once more and express your sadness that you were not able to make amends in a suitable way. Most people who visit these websites are able to read between the lines and tell the difference between a genuine complaint and a person who's just venting off unnecessarily. If he is rude, obnoxious or threatening report him to the website and they will take it from there. The worst perpetrators will usually be blocked out from their account.

However bad it gets <u>never</u>:

- Argue with or insult the writer

- Tell them they are wrong

- Deny the accusation

Mystery or Requested Reviews

Recently, I was delighted to have the opportunity to interview Kim Tasso, a highly-respected professional services marketing consultant who also moonlights as a restaurant and attraction reviewer for <u>www. allinlondon.co.uk</u>, the capital's second largest review website. During our chat, Kim gave me the inside track on how the restaurant reviewing process works from the reviewer's perspective. By the time we'd finished, I felt like my eyes had been illuminated to several fantastic opportunities for restaurants that are looking for better online reviews.

To follow are Kim's top ten tips for restaurants who want to optimise their chances of getting a better review:

1. **Watch out for Mystery Reviewers**
   To start with, Kim explained how most restaurant reviews are conducted by 'Mystery Reviewers'. A mystery reviewer will not make themselves known to the restaurant and will conduct the review as a normal paying customer. To make sure these mystery reviews go as well as possible, it's important to brief your front of

house team to watch out for the signals that could indicate that you have a 'mystery reviewer' in the house. Kim suggests you watch out for anyone writing notes whilst they eat. If you see someone making notes directly on to your menu that could be an even bigger signal that you have a mystery reviewer as a diner. If you see someone behaving this way, make absolutely sure to check in with them early to see if they are happy with their food and service. Waiters should be briefed to point out a potential 'mystery reviewer' to their general manager or supervisor, so he or she can also make a point of checking in on the diner. You don't need to query their behaviour necessarily, but it's best to be vigilant by providing the best service possible. Otherwise, you could miss an opportunity to impress from the start.

2. Ask for a Review

Did you know that some review sites such as All In London invite restaurants to ask for a review? If you've not been reviewed yet, make sure to take advantage of this opportunity. For example, on www.allinlondon.co.uk, go visit the website's Get Listed page and ask a reviewer to come visit using the online form provided. Whatever city or area you're based in, see if there is a local review site that offers the same deal. It might open up opportunities for a review that you never knew existed.

3. Don't Dictate the Date and Time of the Review

Don't assume you can set a time and date for the review that suits your business. Reviewers may not take kindly to being asked to only come at certain times as they may have another day job to attend to and only have availability in the evenings or weekends. Also, reviewers often prefer to see what the venue is like at peak hours.

4. Be Prepared for the Reviewer's Visit

If you've requested a review, the reviewer may be happy to let you know when they are planning to visit. If this is the case, make sure your team is ready to welcome the reviewer and offer assistance when they arrive. Kim explained that she'd had experiences where a PR may have set up the review on behalf of the restaurant and then the team at the venue were not briefed about her arrival. This scenario doesn't reflect well on the restaurant and it could cause embarrassment for the reviewer as he or she has to make an effort to verify their credentials.

5. **Be Helpful During the Review**

There are a number of things you can do to help the review run more smoothly on the day. At the start, present the reviewer with a menu that they can use to write notes on. Be prepared to share information about your best or most popular dishes with the reviewer when they order. At the end of the meal, the manager should make a point to check in with the reviewer and ask if they can provide any further information about the menu and the restaurant. For example, explain what type of customer the restaurant is targeting. Let the reviewer know if you have a particular sales point that gives you a point of differentiation. Perhaps you have a family-friendly focus or dogs are welcome in the bar area at weekends. This is all useful data that can help to make the final review more informative to readers and potential customers.

6. **Be Prepared for Issues**

If the reviewer makes a complaint about something during the meal, make sure that the complaint doesn't go ignored. Unfortunately, Kim recollected that there were a number of occasions when she or her companion complained about something and the issue was not dealt with or not reported back to someone more senior. Really, this should never happen to any customer, but it could have especially damaging consequences when it happens to an influential reviewer. All front-of-house staff members need to be trained to deal with customer complaints in a proactive way.

7. **Ask about Scoring**

Some reviewers will simply give you an overall score out of ten or five. To help understand your final score, ask the reviewer what their scoring system is, so you can better interpret your final published score.

8. Make it Complimentary but Don't Forget the Bill

The general rule is that the reviewer and their companion will not pay for the meal, unless it's a mystery review. Reviewers aim to write about a typical customer experience, so it's highly unlikely that they are going to ask for your most expensive dishes and to drink the bar dry. However, even though the meal is complimentary, the reviewer will still want to see the bill at the end of the meal. This information may be used when scoring the value rating, so it's essential that it's provided. Kim explained that this point is not always clear to waiting staff, who get confused when a bill is asked for from a reviewer. Make sure your FOH team is clear on this point in advance, so they don't need to confuse the issue on the day.

9. If it all Goes Wrong, Discuss it

What if you end up with a negative review? All is not lost according to Kim. If you have a serious complaint about a review, or you feel the review caught you on a particularly bad day then get in touch with the website editorial team. Calmly explain the scenario from your perspective. Ask if it's possible to do another review. You may be surprised to find that you get a second chance, or the original review may be taken down if you have argued your case well. It's certainly worth opening a dialogue which could also help you to get on better terms with the editorial team for the future.

10. Promote your Reviews

If you've been blessed with a great review, then make sure to tell everyone about it. Stick it on your website, tweet about it and Facebook it. I'd like to add to Kim's comment that if you photograph or screen grab your review and post it in your Facebook photo library, it's likely to get more views over time. If you just post a website link for the review, it's likely to get lost in the social media hurly burly within a few days. An image of the review saved to your Facebook album or blog will be easier to find for the future and helps keep your star performance front of mind.

Online Reservation Websites

In an ideal world, your customers would just walk in the door or pick up the phone and make a direct reservation for a table at your venue. There would be no third party fees to pay and your Gross Profit would stay balanced on the healthy end of the scale. However, as we all know, that's just not the way things swing these days. Online reservation websites such as OpenTable.com or toptable.co.uk in the UK, Bookatable.com, livebookings.co.uk and Lastminute.com have become very popular with customers. Their powerful search engines allow the customer to choose by area, type and price within a couple of clicks and results also come up with customer star ratings and news of special offers. From the customer's perspective, this is one of the easiest ways there is to research a venue and make a booking.

Many of these reservation sites also partner with other leading review websites so your listing puts you in the view of many more people who are researching options for their next meal out online. Online restaurant review websites often allow for the inclusion of a link to an online booking page. If this has not been setup and other restaurants on the website have sorted this out, the customer could be led to believe that the restaurant isn't so hot on online customer service. Is this the signal you want to send out to your prospective customers?

Of course, if you're already going great guns with your business you may not want to give away a slice of your receipt to a third party. However, it's also worth bearing in mind that the strongest businesses provide multiple paths to purchase. Not everyone behaves the way we want them to. Some customers will definitely favour this route over all others, so make sure you don't miss out on this business by discounting this option outright. Ultimately, hospitality businesses will usually do much better financially if they push to fill the house rather than holding out to sell fewer covers at the right price.

Discount Voucher Websites

I could say plenty about discount websites such as <u>Groupon</u> and <u>LivingSocial</u> who want to cut a deal with you to offer a meal or drinks offer to their email subscribers for a significant discount. But perhaps I'll stay on the right side of polite and try not to say too much at all! I believe, if you are following my tribe building strategy to the T, you will never need to get involved with these sort of shenanigans. I want to help you attract customers without cutting a deep and unnecessary hole into your business profit. When you are getting everything else right, it will be much easier to resist the temptation to bribe customers in the door with two-for-one offers, free drinks and all the rest.

++++++

Now you have the inside track on how to connect with your tribe online, it's time to step outside your venue and measure up the ways you can engage with your customers from the street to the table.

CHAPTER 5

Attract Visiting Customers to your Tribe

First Impressions

Did you know that most people are able to make an instant judgement of a new person within seconds of meeting? To prove the point, Malcolm Gladwell recounted a psychological experiment in his international best seller *Blink*. In his introductory chapter, he described how psychologist Nalini Ambady showed video tapes of different teachers to a group of students. During the viewing, the sound was turned down and each tape sequence lasted for only two seconds. At the end of the experiment she asked the students to grade the effectiveness of each teacher and then she compared their scores with the effectiveness scores taken from students who had studied under these teachers all term. Amazingly, the results were remarkably consistent between both groups.

Of course, it's not just people we judge in an instant. Your venue could be lucky to get as much as a few second's notice when a new customer passes by at street level. It doesn't matter whether a customer decides to casually stop by or is coming to you for the first time following a recommendation; his first view of your exterior will be immediately stored to memory and in time will contribute to his overall mental picture of your venue.

So what does your venue say on first arrival? It's so easy after being in business for a while to forget to regularly reassess the appeal of your venue exterior. When I initially started to work for Towercrest, the very first thing I did was an exterior review of their flagship London venue Platform Bar & Restaurant. Platform was located on Tooley Street in a railway arch nestled right underneath Platform 1 of London Bridge station. The street is a noisy, bustling thoroughfare that it often log-jammed with buses and commercial vehicles coming to and fro from the City of London. On both sides of the street, there are several bars, restaurants and tourist venues such as the highly popular London Dungeons. Outside every neighbouring venue there are also big, bold wall signs and boards promoting offers and daily specials. When I first started, my client Tony had emphasised that his main objectives were to attract more diners and to encourage people to use the upstairs dining floor. The bar had been more of a success from their launch, but Tony still wanted to see if he could steer the venue back to his original vision. He wanted Platform to be known not just as a bar, but as a great eating out destination offering British, seasonal and sustainably-sourced food in a relaxed and friendly atmosphere. For the business, the big customer opportunity came from the thousands of professional services office workers who were headquartered nearby on the Southbank of the River Thames and worked for multinational names such as PWC, Norton Rose and Ernst & Young. Catching the attention. of these well-heeled local workers needed to be one of Platform's top marketing priorities.

However, the review quickly brought up several issues that needed to be addressed. To start with, there was no signage outside the venue to indicate what was on offer. This was in stark contrast to the highly signed venues Platform was surrounded by. The menu box was attached to the wall beside the front door rather than on the street-side black iron fence at the front of the venue exterior. This meant the passer-by had to go off path and approach the doorway under to get a glimpse of the menu. There was no booking, website or social media information in clear view. In fact, the venue looked totally anonymous. It was incredible that so many people had already managed to make it through the doors. As soon as I shared the results, the team were banging their foreheads in recognition of the issues. Unfortunately, it's all too easy for even the most experienced professionals to miss what's going on outside the venue when the majority of your time is focused on running the business from within the venue walls.

After the review, it didn't take long before we had addressed most of these issues with a series of quick fixes. Firstly, we created wall fixed signage for either side of the front door that described the offer more clearly and provided clear contact details plus details of Platform's Facebook and Twitter accounts. In order to grab the attention of our ideal customer, we made sure to mention that there was 'sustainably sourced, seasonal food' on offer and the cocktails included 'homemade syrups and infusions'. These points were all little cues to attracting tribe members who wanted an ethical, homemade, quality food and drink option. The menu box was reattached to the street-side fence. Photographs were added to the menu box display showing the passer-by the ground and upper floor interiors along with beautiful shots of dishes and cocktails. The Sustainable Restaurant Association logo was more prominently displayed (another important cue for our potential tribe members about the values backing the business). A hanging logo was fixed to the exterior and two blackboards were fixed at a side angle at both exterior ends enabling the manager to promote weekly cocktails and menu specials. Once in use, the boards were updated daily and included lots of chatty lines about the day and the weekly specials. The cocktails board promoted inventively named cocktails mentioning luscious, handmade ingredients. The friendly tone of the boards set another cue for the vibe on offer inside the venue. At last, Platform was ditching the issues of the anonymous exterior. Now, customers were stopping in their tracks and making the decision to step inside.

So what would be the result if you were to examine your own venue exterior? What signals do you think it's currently sending out to passers-by and are they the signals you want to send? If you feel like you need to do an exterior review, you can work through the following check list to help you check if you are presenting your business contact information, features and services to best effect.

Exterior Review Checklist

Venue Entrance / Exterior Checklist	Status	Action
Booking phone number		
Social Media account names		
Website address		
Menu display		
Special Offers or menus		
Restaurant Accreditation:- e.g. - Michelin - TripAdvisor - Hardens		
Service features information:- e.g. - Groups and parties - Open for brunch, lunch, dinner, late night - Private parking		
Food and drink, provenance:- e.g. - craft beers - organic - homemade - authentic Thai - bread baked in house		
Awards		
Reviews		
General wear-and-tear		

Make sure everything is up-to-date. Remove anything that seems past its time. For example, restaurant reviews that are more than two years old should be removed. Reading between the lines customers may think you're not doing so well if you have to rely on five year old praise to sell your business.

However, here's a note of caution. It won't always be appropriate to overload your business entrance with a barrage of messages. If you are an upmarket fine dining establishment or a highly branded chain, then you will want to have less visual clutter around your entrance. If you are a niche business that is aimed at the more visually literate, design focused customer then you will use more subtle design and interior cues to attract your ideal tribe member's attention. On the other hand, if you are heavily dependent on attracting the casual passer-by, and your marketing is more main stream, then you will be wise to provide plenty of obvious visual cues for your customer as to what they can expect inside.

How many times a month do you check your exterior? Or when was the last time you did so? I recently watched a documentary on the BBC about Claridges, the world famous 5-star hotel and restaurant, and noticed with interest that the hotel management team did a weekly check of the building exterior. Every paint scuff, crooked wire or ailing plant was noted and added to the fix list. I figure that's a habit every venue would do well to copy in order to ensure your business is always looking at its best as exteriors have a real and immediate impact on people's purchasing decisions.

Meeting and Greeting

As soon as your customer walks inside the door, you've typically only got another minute to entice the new visitor to stay. A lot of experts may say at this point that your customer is going to be attracted to the décor, or the music or they are salivating at their expectations of the menu or what's behind the bar. I believe however, that your potential tribe member will have an even more heightened impression of your venue. Remember, tribe members like to connect. They like to meet like-minded people. They like to share good news with their friends. They are far more likely to be social than your average customer. As soon as she enters the room, she's going to scan the people in the room. Can she see any people who look like-minded to her? Do the customers look happy and relaxed? If she's waiting to be seated, has someone noticed her? Is she being greeted with a smile? Is that smile a false one or a genuine grin? What's the venue energy like? Does she feel like she'll be attended to or ignored? All of these hyper-quick observations lead to a gut instinct judgement that is made in a flash. If the vibe feels bad, she won't stop to be seated and she will simply walk straight back out the door. If she's made an initial positive judgement only then will she take time to consider the décor and the menu.

So what can you do to make sure that the entrance experience is the best it can be? I believe it just boils down to three key things:

1. Meet and greet your customer within a minute

2. Make your customer feel at home with a genuine smile and a helpful approach

3. And, lastly, but most importantly, encourage your team to engage with guests on arrival. If you've got the right people in place, they'll drop all sorts of 'tribe' clues in the way they speak and interact with your guests.

Okay, the above doesn't necessarily sound like rocket science but the benefits of taking this simple approach can still be very powerful. For example, about six weeks after Le Truc opened, Tony and Kieran, his in-house marketing manager spent a few hours observing how new customers were being greeted by the front of house team on their arrival. The following week, Tony described to me how he felt he had to sit on his hands as he noticed that several customers were left waiting for far too long on arrival and when they were taken to their table he felt the greeting wasn't up to the standard of 'loveliness' he was looking to communicate in all his restaurants . The following day, we had a regular management meeting and we took the time to make a big point about the apparent lack of attention being given to meeting and greeting the customers. As a new venue, Tony believed it was highly important at this point to provide the best possible greeting to each new customer who took the trouble to come through the doors.   As a long-time restaurateur, he knew from past experience that the customer wants to be treated nicely more than just about anything else. Customers will forgive slow service and even mediocre food as long as the greeting is warm, the service is professional and any issues are acknowledged immediately.

To rectify the issue, we asked the manager to make 'meeting and greeting' a top priority for the following 21 days. He needed to repeat this message in his team-briefing every day and ensure that the standard was being raised. Thankfully, it wasn't long before the customers started raving about the friendly staff at Le Truc. Just to prove the outcome of the exercise, here are a few review samples that I've taken from recent TripAdvisor reviews on the Le Truc service standard.

1 'We talked to the three customer facing staff who were all engaging and friendly. We'd certainly go again.'

2 'A warm greeting began our experience; the excellent bartender (whose name we didn't get) from my first visit created us another round of bespoke drinks - seriously, this guy must either read nothing but cocktail books or he's a creative genius (and charming too!). We sat down, surrounded by art and happy tables. Our waitress (Anna) was attentive without being overbearing, and such a nice young girl.'

3 'The fact the team were able to make our dining experience so enjoyable (in a business 3 months old(!)) is a testament to their skill and they should be very proud of what they do here. Can't wait to come back again!'

So, not only did the customers notice the difference, but our happy new tribe members also wanted to tell the rest of the world! This felt like a big win for the business at this early point in its inception. From a tribe-building point of view, I think the compliment about being 'engaging' is particularly important. Engagement builds further on the initial experience of friendliness and helps introduce your customers to your particular 'tribe mindset'. In Le Truc's case, the team came across as friendly, creative, knowledgeable and discerning.

I also believe the above tactics will be much easier to implement if you recruit waiters, bar staff and managers for attitude first and skills or expertise second. A warm and welcoming approach needs to be second nature to your front of house team and it is something that needs to be sustained even when the pressure is on. A respectful work environment will certainly help bring out the best in people and make them feel more happy and relaxed. Some one-to-one coaching can also help people to work on their behaviour issues if they are proving a problem in this regard. However, if you have staff members who seem to be in a bad mood whatever the situation, then it is best to keep them well clear of customers and probably your whole team if you want a smooth running ship. They can have such a negative effect on sustaining that all-important welcoming vibe so do carefully consider people's attitude before putting them front of house.

Let your Interiors do the Talking

Your interior also plays a big role when it comes to grabbing the attention of potential tribe members. As well as the more obvious appeal of the styling, colour scheme and furnishings, what elements of the environment can be used to send cues to your tribe members? As an example, let me share a little story about Leila's Café, which I discovered on a recent Sunday afternoon amble in Shoreditch with my partner Victor. As we approached, the café appeared to have a very unassuming exterior. A few steps closer and I could see there were some interesting looking coloured stools and wooden tables for smokers and al fresco diners. Through the window it looked busy but I could see there were a few free places close to the counter. Everyone in the café looked relaxed and the staff gave off an engaged, busy energy. There were gorgeous-looking home make cakes and Italian fancies piled up on the antique counter. Once we were seated, you could see straight through to the kitchen area where there were dozens of pans and kitchen implements hanging by metal hooks from an overhead rack. On the back wall there was a large Victorian dresser with a plate rack that was now being used to store the little wooden serving boards that acted as plates for their delicious homemade sandwiches and gigantic slabs of Christmas Panetonne. There was a communal white enamelled butter dish with a big slab of dented butter sitting in the middle of the long table we shared with four other people. The knife reminded me of one my Grandmother used to use to butter my toast when I was a little girl in rural Ireland. On a blackboard in one corner, there was a breakdown of the geographic source of ingredients in one of their meals, I guess made in an attempt to make customers more aware of the travel miles incurred by that example meal. On the sound system, there was some violin music playing very quietly in the background. In the far corner, there was a book shelf displaying only four book titles which appeared to have been chosen with care. One was a Penguin book entitled *Ill Fares The Land* by Tony Judt, which turned out to be a highly rated, philosophical essay that makes the case for a return to real values in politics. Victor was curious about the book shelf and after a quick browse he decided to buy a copy of Judt's book.

On leaving the café we realised there was a sister shop next store selling organic and sustainable sourced products that were used as ingredients for the meals on offer at the café. Victor bought two handsome looking fresh artichokes which we took home and had as a special little starter to our evening meal. Without having to say a word, the proprietor had sent out a gushing stream of messages about the values at play behind this business. After 30 minutes we had both checked out with a highly visual and visceral experience stored in memory. After a few sips of perfectly brewed tea, I felt like I wanted to share. I took a photograph of the giant slab of Panetonne we were soon to eat together and then I went on to share that with my friends on Facebook, Twitter and Instagram. I knew other friends would love what they have to offer and frankly, I couldn't wait to return. This was no ordinary cup of tea and piece of cake experience; it was really something special, something evocative of past gentler times whilst also being in complete alignment with values that matter to me now. There were no inflated price tags either. It simply felt like a delightful experience set at a decent price. We shall definitely be back.

Leila's Café is just one particular case in point. I've drawn it in fine detail for you to show how lots of seemingly small things can come together to make a highly memorable customer impact. Many other elements can be used to send connection cues out to your ideal customer. Here are just a few ideas you may want to consider:

What do you Want your Environment to Say to your Tribe?

What do you want your venue environment to say?	Tactics
Relax	Relaxing music, soft colours, comfortable furniture, soft acoustics, herbal teas, space between customers, free newspapers to browse over brunch
Have fun	Use stimulating visuals, break the rules with your décor e.g. graffiti signage, a ping pong table or games on offer
Be stimulated	Choose unusual furniture, use brighter colours, include elements of performance in your presentation, put your kitchen on show, share books and show posters. Exhibit modern art by local artists, upbeat tunes on the sound system
Feel good about your choices	Use recycled furniture and plates, crockery and cutlery. Serve teas, coffees and cold beverages that are fair trade or organic. Recycle waste. Offer charity giving with your bill
Support new ways of doing things	Integrate new technologies into your customer service. Waiters use handheld mobile devices for taking orders
Be pampered	Hand towels at the table, little chocolates with your receipt, quality toiletries in the WC, plenty of flowers and verdant plants, a comfortable environment, luxurious fittings
Enjoy with your friends	Provide seating areas for groups. Provide sharing platters or serving jugs for drinks
Be nostalgic	Dress your venue with period or retro style fittings. Have a nostalgic music playlist. Use old-fashioned smelling toiletries in the W.C., use antique cups and saucers
Support your local community	Share community notices, use local ingredients and display the packaging

At the Table

The Menu

If you want to send a straight and true message to your tribe, look no further than your menu. With a few carefully chosen words your menu can speak volumes. For a clear-cut example of how a few words can immediately set the tone of your business, we need to look no further than the menu for Meat Liquor, the West End's infamous dirty burger and cocktail joint that has had punters queuing around the block these past few years.

At the top of the menu the word 'Meat' appears splattered across the page. Below, the food options are subdivided into Fries, Birds, Bulls, Rabbit Food and Sweet Stuff. Just a few words, but you immediately get the irreverent attitude wafting off the page. Under 'Fries' the menu adds 'Not chips'. 'Simple as, this is the way we roll here', is the loud and clear message. Many of the biggest tribes have cocky gang leaders and in this case, Meat Liquor has taken to this role with gusto and is benefitting from it big time. Simultaneously, they are also members of The Sustainable Restaurants Association. Ultimately, the Neanderthal attitude is a bit of an act. The Meat Liquor team totally understands that people like to play out roles sometime, just to let off steam. The Liquor menu takes that one step further. If you're easily offended, I suggest you jump through to the next page, otherwise read on. Here's the menu's description of their Rose wine. 'Le Nuage Rosé is from the very correct Loire Valley. Don't worry. It's not up its own arse. You can't fuck with rosé. If you mess around it tastes shite. This is fresh and juicy. A proper session wine.' Of course, I'm not advocating this approach for most establishments, but in this case, it's so wrong, it's right if you know what I mean.

Other Soho establishments have resurrected the once-buried tradition of the hand-written menu. I recently posted an example of one such menu from Wardour Street's Duck Soup on Pinterest.com and it got more shares and comments than any other single image I had uploaded to date. This reminded me of the fact that interesting looking menus have the potential to go viral on social media and be seen by far more people through image sharing. Duck Soup's ethos is to offer the sort of food you might expect at a fine dining restaurant, but they have stripped away all the expensive fittings and the need to make reservations. The wine list is also hand written with black marker on a wall of simple white kitchen titles. The recipes and wines are all top notch, but the delivery is understated and accessible to a much broader audience. The first time I ate there I can remember seeing suited and booted professionals in their forties sitting beside faux fur clad clubbers with a small group of Fred Perry attired twenty somethings sitting further along the bar.

Make Your Menu Memorable & Shareable

Here are my top 5 tips for creating a menu that gets talked about and shared:

1. **Be Unique**

   Use words and phrases that may not be expected. Avoid clichés that make no impact.

2. **Keep it Simple**

   Don't clutter your menu with too many options and too much additional information.

3. **Provenance**

   Mention the provenance of your ingredients, especially if they are locally sourced.

4. **Give it More Human Appeal**

   Handwrite specials options and present on blackboards or tiles. If appropriate, add a witty intro to help raise a smile.

5. **Tweet Photos of your Menu**

   Photograph and share your weekly hand-written menus or specials on Twitter or Facebook. Get a member of the team to hold the menu if it's a large board and to appear in shot for an added human appeal.

As well as the menu, there are several other marketing initiatives that you can use to help you connect with your tribe at the table.

Feedback cards

Feedback cards offer your customers a channel to get in touch and let you know how they enjoyed their meal. They also send out the right signal to your tribe as they can see you want to hear from customers. I particularly like this example of a feedback card from The Draft House which asks customers to score with marks out of ten for quality of beer, deliciousness of food and efficiency and warmth of service. They also throw in a nice bit of humour with a 'Generation Game' reference to 'Scores on the Doors'. A simple but engaging piece of marketing.

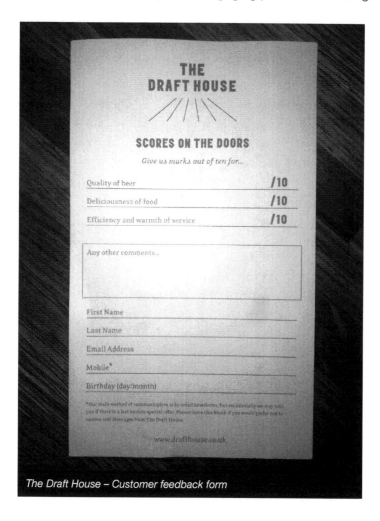

The Draft House – Customer feedback form

Loyalty programme signup

With the advent of Internet-based Customer Relationship Management solutions, electronic loyalty cards are now much easier to set up and to administer for an affordable monthly subscription fee. Again, the presence of a loyalty scheme makes it clear that you want to reward customers for their on-going custom which is another great signal for your tribe. Over time, loyalty cards can help you to build up a valuable database of customer contact information which will be worth its weight in gold as a means for future customer communication.

Receipt

These days even receipts can be used to present messages to your customers. Many chain restaurants now include a web link at the bottom of every receipt inviting customers to send feedback of the venue to an impartial agency. This shows an extra level of integrity when it comes to gathering the customer's feedback. I also love this example from The Table Café that includes an extra big mention of their Facebook and Twitter addresses. This is such a simple, yet effective way to invite customers to connect.

The Table Café - Social Media addresses on receipt

Using Events to Connect with your Tribe

Whether you are the 'host with the most' or a participating player, events can prove to be a fantastic way to attract and engage with your tribe in venue and locally. Coming back to the principals of tribe-building, your tribe will be looking for ways to communicate with you, to meet and make connections with like-minded people and they will want to share in your successes. With a little bit of thought, your events can be created to meet your tribe member's desire for one or all of these experiences. Here are some examples of events that work particularly well in this context:

Food & Drink Festivals

In recent years, indoor and outdoor food & drink festivals have had a real renaissance here in the UK. With a growing interest in ingredients and techniques, these festivals provide a great platform for demonstrating your business's unique take on food and drink. People who love food totally relish these events as they get an opportunity to try out lots of dishes, buy products to take away and learn some new tricks from the professionals. If you can get a demonstration opportunity, grab it with both hands as it can be a fantastic way to raise the profile of both your star players in the kitchen and your business. Allow people to taste samples of your food and drink. Do everything you can to encourage people to talk to you and ask questions about what you do.

As an example, Platform Bar & Restaurant applied for a chance to pitch up at Feast, a foodie event in Guy's Hospital Quad that was recently voted one of the UK's top food festivals. Luckily, the venue was only a short walk from the restaurant so it was an ideal way to get in front of customers who might not have previously visited our venue around the corner on Tooley Street. The festival entrants were screened by the organisers, so Platform's successful entrance at the event also helped to raise their profile with the London foodie scene. As an added bonus, it was a great event to tweet about and to show off Rich the chef's tasty slow braised middle white pig's cheeks with homemade cider and apple sauce.

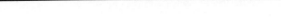

Platform Bar and Restaurant – Photos from FEAST at London Bridge

FEAST warm up on Twitter

Collaborative Events

With collaborative events, I believe you have the potential to create a fizzle of white marketing heat when you put two complementary and like-minded partners together. Think about it. What would Brad Pitt be without Angelina Jolie, or Elizabeth Taylor without Richard Burton?

I watched this thought play out for real when I recently caught the second episode of the BBC's documentary on Claridge's Hotel. Over sixty minutes, I watched with fascination as the story unfolded about the hotel's collaboration with Noma, the Danish restaurant voted 'World's Best Restaurant' by *Restaurant* magazine for the past three years. Here were two international names coming together to create a 10-day pop-up restaurant offering an unrivalled gastronomic experience for their guests and visitors during the London 2012 Olympics. The extraordinary menu included crudités in edible soil, live ants and a 48-hour cooked neck of lamb served on a plate of burning hay. Despite having no more than 3,000 or so covers available over the 10 day period, they had up to deal with upward of 20,000 booking requests. Even by Claridge's standards, this event had an extraordinary and unprecedented demand. For sure, most of us do not have Claridge's or Noma's reputation to pull on, but we can still take inspiration from their creativity.

Taking another much less lofty example, in 2012 Platform's chef competed in the annual Scotch Egg Challenge run by The Ship in Wandsworth, in South West London. The Ship's event organisers had invited up to twenty separate restaurant & bar or gastro pubs to compete at a live cooking event where twenty unique versions of this pub food classic were to be dished up and judged. The event was watched on the night by a rammed packed house full of excited young Londoners. As well as a judge tasting, Scotch egg samples were delivered out to the guests on the floor throughout the night. By the end of the evening, there were scenes reminiscent of a rugby scrum as the tipsy revellers clamoured for a few final samples. It was a bit of a crazy night but an enjoyable and memorable one nonetheless. The Ship also did incredible business that evening, showing again that with a little bit of imagination and a few like-minded collaborators you can make a real business impact with an event and simultaneously draw your tribe closer.

Tasting Evenings

If you offer regular seasonal menus or, for example, if you want to trial the meals you have planned for Christmas season, why not invite some of your best customers to try out your dishes in exchange for feedback. I've seen Platform use this format to very good effect as a reward to customers who provided us with previous comments given on an online questionnaire that was distributed to the customer database by email. At the tasting event, Platform's owner Tony joined the customers where he spent more time chatting with the guests and inviting additional face-to-face feedback. This event provided Tony and his team with further useful insights that were then folded back into the on-going sales and marketing business plan.

Demonstrations and Classes

Ping Pong, the West End dim sum restaurant chain, regularly host dim sum classes and demonstration events which have proved very popular with regular customers and foodies alike. Have you got something you could demonstrate or teach at an in-venue event? If you're a major on cocktails, a Cocktail Masterclass or demonstration showcase could be packaged as a special event booking for couples or small groups. You don't need a special closed-off space. A dedicated area of your bar on a quiet night could become a very suitable location for a small event like this.

Celebrations

Your tribe will want to follow your progress and help you celebrate your successes, so why not celebrate your anniversaries or special occasions with a party or a themed event? Dependent on how generous you're feeling, you can either make it a ticketed affair or welcome selected people as your guests on the night. Whatever you do, publically acknowledge and thank people for their support. Take the time to call out your stars and introduce them to your guests. Tribe members will be curious to meet the chef and the people behind the scenes. Remember to include all your team members in the congratulations as a tribe is first and foremost a team. If only a few egos are praised, the positive effects of a celebration could backfire in the longer term.

Charity Fund-raisers

If your business is associated with a local good cause, or you want to help to raise funds for a bigger social campaign, why not create a supporting event that you can host at your venue? As an example, whilst Platform were at their London Bridge venue, they hosted two annual birthday bashes which showcased talented performing youngsters from local youth development charity XLP. At the height of the evening, the mike was handed over to the charity founder, Patrick Regan, and he was given an opportunity to talk about their work helping young people to rise above difficult personal circumstances in South East London. Tribes love businesses with a vision. If you have a desire to support local social initiatives or charities, an event could provide the perfect platform to help your cause and to say something that matters to your audience.

++++++

I believe you will need to focus all of your marketing attention on three key areas if your tribe-building marketing strategy is to succeed. We're already covered the first two important factors 1) online communications and 2) initiatives which will attract your potential tribe members when they visit or come across you at events. Now we're going to look at the final piece in the jigsaw – the people who help you deliver your business, or as I like to call them, your dream team.

CHAPTER 6

Your Marketing Dream Team

Your Management Team

One of the main things that has driven me to write this book is the desire to unlock an important marketing force that usually lies dormant within a business. I see too many businesses assume that marketing is the sole responsibility of the marketing manager. In the worst cases, the owner also removes herself from the process with the excuse that she is too busy looking after everything else. I believe, for a Tribe-building strategy to truly succeed, everyone needs to have a hand in making it happen. I'm not saying that everyone needs to spend several hours a week exclusively focused on marketing activities. What's important here is that everyone understands the objectives of the marketing plan and what particular part they can play to help make it happen.

The Boss

It's your roll to make marketing a business priority and to ensure that the right resources are allocated to make your business success a reality. You'll have final say on the team, the strategy and the marketing budget. More importantly, from the perspective of building your tribe, it's also your role to walk and talk your brand values. Your leadership should reflect how these values play out on a day-to-day basis in your business. If you're quality-focused, you'll need to show you care about the small things. Do you give people honest, respectful feedback when you see standards slipping. If you've emphasised 'teamwork' as one of your brand values, you won't be able to use a 'Command-and-Control' management style and still expect people to buy into your vision. Remember a tribe is not a tribe without a leader, so be prepared to dig deep and reflect on your behaviour and its impact. The world is crying out for leaders who can step forward with integrity and commitment to their values. Take this road and I guarantee the outcome will be a win-win for both you and your business.

Strategic Business & Marketing Advisors

Ok, hands-up, I have a vested interest here in getting you to include a business and marketing advisor as part of your team. If you feel happy that you've got the best brains to hand when it comes to marketing and running your business, then you can keep your strategic marketing planning activities in-house. However, if you wonder whether you've got the right approach or if you're struggling in any way to make a return from your existing marketing efforts, it's highly advisable to get some support and insight from outside your business.

You can call on an independent marketing consultant or a marketing agency for this role. Firstly, I'd advise that you find someone who already has some experience of your niche or sector. Secondly, can he give you examples of tangible positive results delivered to other businesses in the past year? Is your advisor up-to-date with the latest marketing technologies and social media? If he starts a conversation with you by saying that marketing is a numbers game, where it's all about reaching x hundred thousand people in order to secure the number of new leads you're looking for, then I'd quickly start looking for the trap door lever. Smart consultants know that these days it's much more about talking to the right people in the right way. It's not about marketing to the masses, it's about marketing to your niche customer group. Buying mega-thousand email or mailing lists off the shelf and sending them out willy-nilly is a waste of money that will result in miniscule levels of customer engagement. Even if your budget is limited, informed advice from an experienced consultant at the beginning of your planning phase will ensure that you don't end up throwing money away on pointless new courses of action.

Marketing Manager

If your business includes three or more venues, it's likely that you'll have put a dedicated marketing manager in place who's responsible for overseeing the marketing of your business on a day-to-day basis. If you've got a single venue it's more likely that you the owner and/or your general manager will carry the brunt of the responsibility for marketing. Whatever your scenario, the important thing here is to make sure your manager knows what tasks he needs to be responsible for and what tasks he needs to prioritise on an on-going basis. Additionally, he needs to be clear about what tasks he should share with other members of the team. Effective delegation and project management are two essential skills that every marketing manager now needs to master. Without them, he will struggle to kick-start the incredible marketing resource that could be lying dormant within your wider team.

I won't beat around the bush here. A tribe-based marketing strategy is going to need plenty of time and effort to get fired into action. However, you're going to spend a lot less money on advertising, email lists, big launch parties and special offer discounts. What you are doing is moving resources and money from where they no longer work to where they will be much better invested. If you hand the responsibility for the delivery of every aspect of tribe-building strategy to your marketing manager or general manager, it's likely that they will quickly burn out and then drop out of your business. I've seen many brave young managers desperately struggle to keep on top of things and finding it enormously stressful in the process.

Not so long ago, and I'm only talking five or six years ago or so, marketing was a much more straight forward discipline where you could have more easily expected to hive off marketing to one department or manager. At that point we didn't have world-wide mass use of Facebook and Twitter. Smart phones were still a rarity. People were reading newspapers in large numbers and a loyalty card was a small piece of cardboard which got a little ink stamp each time you purchased a coffee. Now that world is well and truly gone, everyone is grappling to keep up and that's especially the case with marketing managers. Performance failure becomes an unfortunate reality as your manager struggles to get a grip on all the new technologies never mind actually working out what's the best route to take. I think the solution lies in getting marketing managers to concentrate on what they are best at, and getting other members of the team to support with the tasks that can be managed more easily. Maybe some of you think it would be better to put all your marketing budget in the hands of an external agency. Well that's great if you can afford it, but from what I've seen of the industry to date, most restaurant, bar or café businesses don't want to pay the fees that quality agencies want to charge. The new tribe-building marketing plan is going to be more labour intensive for your in-house team as it's much more focused on building relationships and real engagement. Once you come around to this realisation, then you're in a better position to allocate budget and resources in a way that gets results and doesn't end up with a frazzled marketing manager or assistant high tailing it out the door.

General Managers & Assistant Managers

Your general manager is the man or woman at the front, the person who knows exactly what is going on in your venue on a day-to-day basis. It's difficult for a marketing manager to catch everything that is going on in venue, that's why it's so important for the general manager to become their right-hand ally. For example, if you want to connect with your customers on Facebook and Twitter it's important to show everyone photographs of what's going on in your venue. Make your general manager or your assistant manager responsible for taking photos of your latest dishes and cocktails. Photograph your special offers chalk boards. Get them snapping at special events and parties at your venue. Photograph your in-house team when they're celebrating or entertaining. With proper training on social media, you can also enable your managers to post straight to Facebook and Twitter so you serve your news to the world as it happens. On social media, most stories are not worth reporting the day after, so getting your front of house team to help capture social news opportunities in the moment is worth its weight in gold.

If you're a multi-venue business, each venue should have a mini-marketing plan which is drafted by the general manager and outlines the marketing strategy and weekly or monthly tactics that will be actioned in that particular location. Coming back to the tribe-building strategy, make sure the mini-plans are aligned with this approach and use tactics that support the creation of a more local tribe. Make sure to avoid a scenario where your head office delivers a new tribe-building strategy which is then not properly understood by the local teams. Education is absolutely essential to ensure the top level plan is echoed in everything you do at ground level. Without education, your local teams may well resort to the old tactics without realising the need to change their ways and come into alignment with the new approach. First you need to ensure your general and assistant managers are fully briefed on new strategy changes and then they will be better able to devise and manage mini-plans that don't clash with the overall approach. Your front of house managers are also there to walk and talk your brand value, setting the tone for what your business stands for on a day-to-day level.

Your Customer Service Team

Chefs, Cooks, Mixologists, Sommeliers and Baristas

No bar or restaurant marketing team would be complete without the amazingly creative people behind the bar and the kitchen pass. These are the guys and girls who consistently deliver your classics and who dream up exciting new recipes and drinks for the delectation of your customers. Your marketing manager will want to work with your food and drink teams to think up innovative new ways to present the highlights from your menu. Food and drink photography is BIG on social media. In a recent survey from the US, it's claimed that 19% of social media consumers now use social media sites when they eat out socially[10]. And more interestingly for UK businesses, a survey published by PC World & Curry's revealed that 65% of customers with smartphones now check their social media updates whilst they're at the restaurant [11]. The most common activities are checking in, posting status updates and uploading photos. Handled well, I think this behaviour offers a fantastic opportunity when it comes to encouraging online chatter about your business direct from the table or bar.

For example, get your teams to think about making your food more photogenic. What little presentation tricks could your team implement to get more people snapping while they eat? A few weeks ago, one of the kitchen staff at Le Truc painted a personalised and pretty looking *'bon anniversaire'* message around the edge of a desert plate in chocolate sauce. And guess what, it got immediately snapped and posted on Twitter by one very happy recipient. Not only do people want to take photos of their food, they also want to look at pictures of your food even before they arrive at your venue. Some people amusingly refer to this trend as foodporn. When customers really get a real kick from eating your food, it's a wonderful little flirtatious act to share photos of your gorgeous food or cocktails for customers to feast their eyes on hours in advance of arrival! So engage your kitchen and bar teams and get them switched on to working with this trend and making it work big time for your business.

Front of House Team

Don't limit marketing involvement and education to only your most senior team members. If you invest in regular social media marketing briefings for your front of house team you can boost the successful delivery of your social media strategies further still. Front of house waiter and bar team members can be invited to think about photo and message opportunities for social media. I also recommend that the marketing manager prints out a list of your top social media fans each week, so the waiting staff know to recognise these special customers when they walk in the door. It's now possible for your marketing manager to use tools like TweetReach to run weekly reports that will indicate exactly who's been talking about you on Twitter in the past week. These reports will show each follower's twitter address and their twitter account photo which can then be distributed to the team for reference. Really get to know and appreciate these Tweeters and it's likely that they will return the love you've shown with more tweets and complimentary posts.

Identify people in your front of house team who could also serve as great ambassadors for your business beyond the venue walls. Invite your team members to represent your venue at business networking breakfasts or lunches. This can be a great way to promote special offers on Christmas dinners or corporate entertainment packages. If you're in an aligned niche, courting corporate customers on a personal basis can make a big difference to the bottom line. Make sure anyone who represents your business is suitably briefed and has a 'social pitch' prepared and practiced that will explain your business's key points of difference within a couple of sentences. For example here's a one minute networking pitch for my client's restaurant Le Truc: *'Hello, I'm ....*
from Le Truc. We're a new independently-owned French restaurant that serves great French classics such as Coq au Vin and Potato dauphinoise in a relaxed and friendly atmosphere. Our venue has been inspired by the spirit of the Birmingham Surrealists and our walls are covered in artworks & sculptures especially created by local Birmingham artists. Our bar tender is award winning and our team are totally dedicated to ensuring your visit will be an enjoyable and memorable one. The next time you have a business lunch or dinner at our restaurant, make sure to hand in this postcard which will entitle you and your guest to a complementary cocktail. We hope you'll come and visit us soon. Thank you from .... at Le Truc.'

Extend a friendly invitation to business people you meet who want to check out your premises for events or group bookings. Make sure the prospective corporate customer knows who to ask for if they come to visit (ideally get them to book an appointment in advance) and make it someone's responsibility to show them around and explain more about what's on offer. This is a fantastic opportunity to make your corporate guest feel special, so make sure your general manager or assistant manager also says hello and offers your visitor a complimentary drink and a friendly handshake. That's a great way to make your mark and to give your prospective customer a fantastic impression of your hospitality.

The contributors to your tribe-building strategy are not just to be found in your venues. There are dozens and maybe hundreds of people you will work with over time who can also have a part to play.

Your Marketing Partners

Copywriter

A great copywriter will help you make an immediate and positive impact on your customers. When it comes to writing copy for websites, menus and flyers, the language will need to be distinctive and concise in order for it to stand out and make an immediate impact. The best copywriter is the one who starts by asking lots of questions. She'll want to understand everything about your customer and your tribe. She'll want to know about your customer demographics, how they spend their free time, their fashion preferences and lifestyle choices. She'll ask you about your business objectives, the vibe and values you want to communicate throughout all your marketing material.

One of her most important jobs is to work out what's the best tone to use when speaking to your customers. For example, one of my client's venues, The Selly Sausage Café is based very close by to Birmingham University. Students make up the large majority of the customers at the café and the tone used across the marketing copy is humourous, streetwise and full of slang. Le Truc, on the other hand has a French hipster vibe and the language is smattered with Franglais and has a hip, playful tone. Setting the tone is incredibly important when building a tribe. The tone is a major indicator of the sort of business you are and it plays an important role in helping to connect with the customer. It sends out a signal that says, 'We're people like you. We understand you and we get what you're all about. In fact, we even sound like you!'

If you've not got the budget for a full-time copywriter, and you don't have good copywriting skills in-house, consider getting a writer to come and work with you on a short project to define and provide examples of how to apply the proposed tone to your marketing collateral on an on-going basis. This short-term investment will greatly improve your chances of connecting with your audience for the longer term. A little investment in copywriting skills and training for your in-house marketing manager can also go a long way, if they are to be responsible for writing your copy on a day-to-day basis.

Interior, Brand & Communication Designers

If you want your visual communications and interiors to say all the right things about your brand you'll need to secure the services of the best designers, branding design specialists and artists that you can afford. Seriously, I believe they are worth the investment. Did you know that businesses that invest in design are significantly more likely to outperform other businesses? According to the Design Council website, the most commonly reported rate of return from companies calculating a percentage return on design investment was 15%[12]. So in effect, investment in a great designer can make a significant contribution to your bottom line. As with the copywriter, the best designers and branding specialists will always ask plenty of questions about your customer and business objectives at the start. Where possible, get someone who has a track record designing for your industry, who understands the visual language that works best for your food and drink customers.

Colour, fonts, styling, fitting design and signature objects all convey meaning that will be picked up by your tribe members. In many instances, your advocate fan will be far more sensitive to the design you utilise than your average passer-by. When Le Truc first opened it received a rather disparaging review from the *Birmingham Post*. The reviewer was particularly perplexed by the interior design. He didn't understand the shabby chic of plain wooden tables and chandeliers and he got particularly miffed by the graffiti style signs for the men's loos. The appeal of the venue design was completely lost on his personal visual aesthetic. He has a tribe-mindset, but he belongs to the wrong tribe. In comparison, the Birmingham food blog, *Dine in Birmingham*, enthusiastically described several of the venue's customised design pieces including the pink papier-mâché poodle bust that hung over the ladies toilets in loving detail. Mr 'Dine in Birmingham' is acting like a fully signed-up Le Truc tribe member. He completely gets what the venue is about and he delights in describing and recounting its every detail.

Dependent on your budget, you can work with a print designer full time, or you can have the designer create templates for your menu, posters, flyers etc that can then be updated by your in-house team for weekly or monthly promotions. For seasonal promotions, it will have more impact if you have a tailored design produced. Christmas dinner bookings for example can bring in much higher revenue than normal. As there is also incredible competition from other restaurants at that time of the year, it's really worthwhile making an extra investment on bespoke copy and design so your business can well and truly stand out from the crowd.

When it comes to both design and copywriting, you want to make sure your designer and copywriter are masters of the three Cs; clarity, coherence and consistency. Look at their previous design work and ask yourself is it easy to understand, is it meaningful in relationship to the wider customer experience and, last but not least, is it consistent with every other piece of marketing material that was designed for that business?

Photographer

More than ever before eye-catching photography has an essential part to play in attracting new tribe members and more run-of-the-day customers alike. The hottest content on social media is photography. Creatively photographed food and drink will get you plenty more clicks, reTweets and shares. Again, think about the style of photography that will send out the right signs to your tribe members. Would black and white or colour work best? How can you reflect the lifestyle preferences of your tribe within the photographs you commission? Brightly coloured photography gets more clicks on social media, so if it's appropriate how can you work with colour as an active, engaging element of your images? Sometimes, your tribe will not respond so well to glossy photos but will respond more favourably to quirky images that display personality and creativity or that tell an engaging story. The photography choices you make should all refer back to the values and brand personality you want to project. Are you cutting edge and cool or approachable and friendly? When you're clear about your brand, it's going to be so much easier to brief your photographer and to get outstanding results.

Party and event photographs are also a must have. Just make

sure to ask for permission to post photos of party or event attendees before you post them on social media. Asking for permission might be drag, but, trust me, it's better to have people's permission as posting photographs from events onto social media channels can bring up all sorts of personal boundary issues if you're not careful. I will not name names, but this story may act as a warning to the consequences of not asking permission. At a restaurant event I attended earlier this year, a customer was photographed interacting with an entertainer during the night's performance. Within the hour, the photograph had been tweeted on the restaurant's Twitter account. However, very shortly afterwards the man's wife tweeted a comment back to say she now knew where her husband was. Unfortunately, the man in question had been attending the event with another woman so it's likely that this particular tweet had rather unfortunately consequences for the customer. Whatever you think of the circumstances, it's not in a restaurant's interest to unduly embarrass or compromise a customer through posted pictures or comments. So it's best to ask in advance to be on the safe side.

Web Developer

All the headlines may be grabbed these days by social media, but you still need a great website to promote your business. Your website does the practical job of providing information about your menus, your location and contact details. It also sends out visual signals as to what your brand is all about through its design, photography and copy tone. Here are a few points to consider when recruiting a web developer to join your dream team.

Beware the developer who comes bearing new technology gizmos. Until recently, it was all the rage to include videos, animations and all sorts of other flashing bits and bobs on a website. Seriously, if you want to include surround videos and flashing animations, think again. Most customers will not thank you for including features that just slow down their route to the information they are seeking out. Get to the point with your website. Make it easy for people to find out what food and drink you serve, how to find you and how to make a booking. Think twice if your web developer suggests a website plan that includes dozens of sections. Maybe you want to include all that brand definition copy about why you do what you do and what you stand for as a business. After tracking website statistics for several years, I can tell you with all confidence that most people don't read that stuff. As they say in the movies, 'don't tell, show'. The brand value planning I covered earlier in the book is to help get you and your team in the right mind-set. For everyone else, the brand values are acted out through the hundreds of ways you do business every day. The only place you may want to talk about your brand values and vision more overtly is in the recruitment section. This is a good place to start connecting with your potential employees and it's appropriate to lay out your values as a business and talk about the sort of people you are looking for in this website section. Make sure your developer can optimise your website for mobile phones and tablets. Mobile internet usage has gone ballistic in recent years, so you absolutely need to have a website that works well on a small phone size screen. This is all the more reason to steer clear of those techno gizmos that have a habit of not functioning well on a mobile Internet browser.

Has your developer offered you a content management system within your website design? Having the ability to upload your new menus and include latest news updates thorough Twitter or Facebook feeds on your home page will cut down your website management costs and also enable you to make more regular updates as you need them.

Web developers can also have skilled SEO advisors on hand to help make your site more visible on search engines. If they can show you evidence of other businesses they've helped, this is one of the best indicators as to whether to commission their services in this area. Alternatively, look for an independent SEO consultant and agency who has even more specialism in this field. Additionally, web developers with in-house design teams can also assist with branding your Facebook and Twitter profiles, so they remain consistent in style with your website. In our digital age, a good web development partner is an essential dream team member and should be chosen with plenty of care and consideration.

Other Supporting Partners

Professional Advisors

Think about how you can encourage your professional service advisors such as your accountants, lawyers and business advisors to become leading advocates for your brand. Through regularly working with you they are going to get to know your business better than most. If you have a good working relationship they are likely to talk about you with their wider network and people in these professions often have very wide networks. Show them some love. Invite them to your special events. Give them a loyalty card that they can use or that their family members can use. I know this can be a bit of an issue with larger firms, but with smaller firms most will be very happy to be treated as extended members of the family. Also, ask for their feedback not just on the aspects of the business they are directly involved with, but on its wider appeal. This deeper engagement will help draw you closer and encourage your professional associates to think and talk more favourably about your business or perhaps even hire your venue for special events and Christmas parties.

Suppliers

Who are your favourite suppliers? It's likely they are not just suppliers, but like-minded people and businesses who care about similar things to your business. Think about how you can celebrate each other's good news and spread the word about each other's services. Twitter is a fantastic channel for this. You might have a specialist cheese supplier who also has a shop in the local area. Get excited about the new cheeses they have introduced you to. In the process you can share information about the provenance of the cheese and you are also supporting a local business. Celebrate when your suppliers have won awards or reached significant milestones. With this approach, everyone wins. Through re-tweets, you can both create awareness of each other's businesses and in the process clock up lots more valuable tribe-building brownie points.

Local Community

Who's on your doorstep? Have you stepped outside and interacted with your local community? A great way to build your tribe is to find local business people who also care about your area and who are looking for ways to make your neighbourhood flourish. Government-based Business Improvement Districts have sprouted up all over the UK and they are always looking for ways to help promote the businesses in their catchment area. Make sure your general manager attends the local meetings and makes an effort to get to know the other local business owners. If you've got a loyalty card scheme make sure you give your local business neighbours a card to encourage their custom. Consider how you might club together with other businesses to attract more customers to your area. As an example, Platform Bar & Restaurant became involved with the Quality SE1 Pub Crawl that was organised in conjunction with several of the other local pubs that served craft or independent beers and ales. Each event was also attended by independent brewers who wanted to showcase special beers on the night. It proved to be a great promotional vehicle for the participating venues and achieved high levels of Twitter activity on the day of the event and on the days running up to it. Coverage didn't just stop at social media. It also went on to win further media coverage in print. For example, the crawl was favourably listed in *Shortlist*, the London-wide free magazine that is distributed to over half a million people each week.

++++++

So the moral of the story so far is, think big when you think about your tribe. Involve everyone possible and you will end up firmly rooting yourself in your community and in the hearts and minds of hundreds and then thousands of your core tribe followers. Of course, getting your dream team on board is just one part of the equation. Next up, we'll look at the essential marketing tools that will help you to develop and keep on top of your customer communications without burning the candle at both ends.

CHAPTER 7

Which Social Media Channels?

Which social media channels should I use to market my business? This must be one of the most common questions I'm currently asked by business owners. With so many channels on offer and more being added to the mix every few months, it's no wonder businesses are confused. In response, I've written the following chapter to give you an insider's view on what works and what doesn't when it comes to engaging with your tribe members and wider audience on each channel.

Twitter

Not so long ago, businesses were still convincing themselves that social media channels like Twitter were only for the followers of blunder-prone Premiership football stars or teeny-bopper fans of the world's biggest R&B and film stars such as Rihanna and Ashton Kutcher. Just in case you're still thinking that might be the case, let me share some recent statistics with you.

Recent figures from Twitter UK, released in May 2012 revealed that there are currently around 10 million active Twitter accounts in the UK and around 80% of these Twitter users accessed the network via their mobile. Around 60% of users are in the 24–45 year old age group. OK, so far, nothing unexpected perhaps. However, I was also interested to read a research report published by Kantar Media TGI in 2011, which noted that around 400,000 British adults over 50 were reported to be using blogs, content-sharing or social media networking websites on their mobile phones. This group were three times more likely to earn £50,000 plus per year than other adult mobile phone owners and they were also 45% more likely to be educated to degree level. The research concluded that Twitter is a key channel to target the wealthy, educated, over 50s[13]. My own experience of Twitter would bear out these conclusions. If you are any sort of mover or shaker in business, Twitter has now become a hugely useful communications tool.

Hospitality Brands on Twitter

A group of the UK's leading chefs have taken to Twitter like a duck to water. For example, Irish chef Richard Corrigan (@corrigansfoods), who is chef-patron at Corrigan's at the Mayfair provides great photos, customer interaction and industry chat on Twitter. The UK's most famous chefs, Gordon Ramsey has over 1.1 million followers and Jamie Oliver clocks in with a whopping 2.7 million followers. It appears the public are becoming ever more ravenous for the latest inside scoop on the opinions and output of their favourite celebrity chefs.

And Twitter is not just for the biggest celebrity names. Whether you're looking for a specialist beer, a mainstream chain, or news and offers from your local café, Twitter has now become the place to get the latest news on daily menus, events, offers, gossip and more. As an illustration, I've put together a chart highlighting some hospitality businesses that are going great guns with their daily 140 character tweets (figures from January 2013).

Example Food & Drink Brands on Twitter	Number of Twitter Followers
Gordon Ramsey - @gordonramsey01	1,193,454
Jamie Oliver - @jamieoliver	2,947,307
Nando's - @nandos_UK	662,712
Jancis Robinson - @jancisrobinson (*The Daily Telegraph's* Wine Expert)	169,749
Richard Corrigan - @corrigansfood	20,806
Yo!Sushi - @YOSushi	25,351
Giraffe - @giraffetweet	24,516
Humming Bird Bakery - @hummingbirdbakery	36,648
Pizza Express - @pizzaexpress	24,949
Mark Hix Foods - @hixrestaurants	19,690
The Dolphin Pub @The_Dolphin_Pub * These guys are a bit explicit with their language so don't look if you're easily offended.	11,148
Cask Pub & Kitchen - @CASK_PUB_SW1	5,033
Draft House - @DraftHouseUK	4,203
The Southampton Arms – @southamptonNW5	3,927

What Can you Do on Twitter?

- Twitter allows you to post text messages of up 140 characters (and that includes spaces).

- You can attach a photograph or video link to any tweet. Most people post photos on Twitter that they have just taken on their mobile phone.

- A tweet (a Twitter message) can also include a website link. These links are usually shortened using a website such as Bit.ly or a Social Media Publishing tool like Hootsuite or Tweetdeck to keep the maximum number of characters free for the tweet text.

- Twitter allows you to pay for and send promoted tweets to Twitter users. The tweets will be sent to people who Twitter think will find your subject of interest, and they can be targeted by country only.

- You can chat with people on Twitter by sending them a tweet. To chat, just include their Twitter name in the tweet (i.e. @contact_name) If the Twitter account holder follows you, you can send them a private tweet which is called a Direct Message or DM for short.

- People can follow conversations on Twitter by searching for mentions of a hashtag. A hashtag will have # sign at the front and will include no spaces. E.g. #QSE1PC is a hashtag used by my client Platform Bar & Restaurant when they want to talk about the Quality SE1 Pub Crawl they organised around London's SE1 district. People who are going on the crawl can include the hashtag in their tweets, so others can search for that hashtag within Twitter to see who else will be attending or they can find out where to catch up with the Crawl group along the way.

- When people want to share your Tweets, they hit the ReTweet button to send your tweet to all their followers. Encouraging ReTweets is a great way to get your message or brand name out to a wider audience.

- Last but not least, independent of whatever you're doing on Twitter people can mention you and your business on Twitter in their independent conversations and posts. For example, they might mention your name, your Twitter address or a hashtag you're using.

What's Twitter Good for?

Your Latest News

Twitter has become THE platform for breaking news. When you write a status update, Twitter asks you 'What's happening?' They used to ask 'What are you doing?' but over time they realised that people were much more interested in sharing and hearing about what you're witnessing right now. The best Tweeters always keep this in mind.

Twitter account – The Eagle in Hoxton

Showcasing your food

Through photo sharing, Twitter is a brilliant tool for showcasing your food. With the right marketing strategies and tactics, you can also encourage customers to photograph and share photos of your food with their wider following.

Customer Feedback and Requests

Given its simplicity, Twitter is becoming the go-to place when customers want to give feedback. If a customer is a tribe member, he wants everyone to know how great you are, so he will want to share praise for your business on Twitter. On the other hand, if he is a disgruntled customer, he can feel more powerful by letting you and all your followers know how unhappy he is with your service or your food. True, it's a double-edged sword. The main thing is that you recognise this trend and deal with it. Proactive, positive engagement always looks attractive.

Some restaurants are now taking reservations on Twitter or even special orders from customers. When you allow customers to communicate with you on their preferred communications channel, you're shouting from the rooftops that you are happy to do things the customer's way. This is where you need to go if you're looking for exceptional customer loyalty.

The Selly Sausage on Twitter for Mobile

Brand Positioning

If you're positioning your brand towards the hipper, trendier or go-getter end of the market, it's absolutely essential that you communicate on Twitter. Your presence here indicates that you understand how your customers like to communicate. Not only that, you know the rules and you have mastered this form of communication. Regular, great quality tweets will give you the brand edge you simply have to display to connect to your desired customers. It's also become an essential brand positioning tool for the biggest casual dining brands such as Nando's (@ NandosUK). Nando's has a broad appeal across all cultures and a big fan base with younger diners. Their brand tone is distinctly cheeky and entertaining and has translated well to their content and entertainment or games-led promotions on Twitter and Facebook.

Connecting with Journalists and the Media

Journalists and the media love Twitter. If you want to make a noise about what you're doing, make sure you follow the key journalists in your sector and make them aware that they can keep updated with your latest news on the channel.

Live Interviews

Live interviews on Twitter are becoming a new way to allow customers to ask questions and to get to know your in-house stars better. To set up a Twitter interview, you invite question tweets during a certain time frame which will be answered live by your special guest or expert. This sort of activity tends to work best when you've got a larger following or a star name who's developing or who wants to develop a media profile

What is Twitter Not so Good for?

Sell, Sell, Sell

Continuous sales messages and promotions will get you nowhere fast on Twitter. It's a social channel, so you must take the time to chat, entertain and inform. The aim is to build relationships, attract and entice. If you publish occasional promotions in the midst of this sort of content, it will be much better received. Even if you are selling, make sure the copy has a social tone.

The Detail

Whatever you say on Twitter, it's got to be short and sharp. Save the longer messages for your blog.

Time poor, Middle of the Road Demographic

Some demographics are less well represented on Twitter. If you're aiming at time-poor, lower-income, middle agers, Twitter is probably not going to be your channel.

Old News

If your news is old, don't bother repeating it on Twitter. As mentioned above, Twitter is all about what's happening now.

Statistics

Unlike Facebook, Twitter account holders are not provided with any statistics about their account on the channel. However, if you are prepared to make some investment you can get user reports and click through reports from Twitter management tools such as Hootsuite or Tweetdeck. For more detailed reports on your Twitter user behaviour, for example how much they retweet or when your followers are most active on Twitter, you can buy a subscription to an online software tool such as www.followerwonk.com which is priced from US$99 per month (2013 price).

Facebook

As of December 2012, there are about 16 million active Facebook users in the UK today with a total of 42.4 million UK accounts registered in total. Think that's big? Globally, the numbers are even more impressive as Facebook now has an incredible 1 billion plus registered Facebook users. Facebook and Twitter may often be mentioned in the same breath, but they really are quite different creatures. For a start, Facebook users spend much longer on the platform. For example, Facebook visits account for 50% of all UK mobile Internet visits. That means one in every two Internet visits on a mobile phone is to Facebook. In social media terms, it's the big daddy of them all.

Demographically, Facebook has fans of every age group with about 51.3% women and the rest men. According to Fanalyzer.co.uk, in December 2012 the UK Facebook fanbase breaks down as follows:

13–1 7 year olds – 13%

18–24 year olds – 24.5%

25–34 year olds – 25.5%

35–44 year olds – 17.5%

45–54 year olds – 11.1%

55–64 year olds – 5.4%

65+ – 3.1%

Hospitality Brands on Facebook

When it comes to hospitality brands on Facebook, it's the big chain names who rule. Nando's stands head and shoulders above the rest, with over 1.2 million fans following its main UK Facebook page. As of December 2012 the top UK restaurant brands on Facebook are:

Nandos – 1.3 million

Pizza Hut UK – 970 K

Just-eat.co.uk – 800 K

Domino's Pizza – 731 K

Toby Carvery – 354 K

At the premium end of the scale the follower numbers are much lower than what you might expect to see on Twitter, for example:

The Fat Duck – 11 K

Marco Pierre White – 8.3 K

Fifteen Cornwall – 7 K

If your business is big into cakes and baking, Facebook is a great place to speak to your customers. Check out the Hummingbird Bakery on Facebook which has over 62,000 signed up to salivate over their gorgeous daily cupcake photos. Night clubs like the Ministry of Sound, themed bars such as the Hard Rock Cafe and prestige private clubs like Soho House also do really well on Facebook. The defining factor for the success of these brands on Facebook is that they don't just offer food and drink. They are also able to layer their offer with entertainment, humour, aspirational, glamorous or prestigious content.

What can you do on Facebook?

Unlike Twitter, Facebook offers an incredibly diverse range of options when it comes to attracting and talking to your customers. In fact, this section alone is probably a book in its own right. However, for all of you who are looking for some help with the basics, here's a whistle-stop guide to some of the major features you can currently use as a business on Facebook.

- Facebook allows all users with a personal profile to set up one or several Facebook business pages.

- You can setup your page as a brand, a company or a location-based business or if you're a well-known name you can set up a celebrity page.

- Several people can be set up as administrators to manage a single or multiple business pages.

- As a Facebook page, you can post regular text updates, photos, video clips or links to anyone who 'Likes' your page.

- Facebook enables business to advertise within the Facebook environment to fans and non-fans alike for a pay-as-you go fee, much like a Google Ad Words account. You can choose who you want to see your ads, by gender, age, location, interests etc. and you can set your budget as you wish.

- Facebook tabs are an add-on feature provided inexpensively by many third-party companies that enable you to create offer pages, integrated menus, newsletter signup forms and table booking from directly within Facebook.

What's Facebook good for?

You can offer visitors much more attractive incentives to follow you on Facebook by adding special offer pages. These offer pages can be added when you subscribe to services such as www.northsocial.com or www.woobox.com or they can be set up for you by your web development or marketing agency.

Giraffe – Facebook App Dinner Winner Promotion

If your content goes viral, i.e. your fans start sharing it and commenting on it in big numbers, you have the potential to reach a much wider audience with friends of your fans also viewing your content. Once you have 30 or more fans on your Facebook page you can start to view your visitor statistics, e.g. how many people visit, the demographics of your audience and on what content your audience engages with most.

acebook fans can also use their smart phone Facebook app to check-in to Facebook pages that are set up as location-based businesses. It's an especially popular feature for customers of restaurants, bars and cafés who want to let friends know where they are.

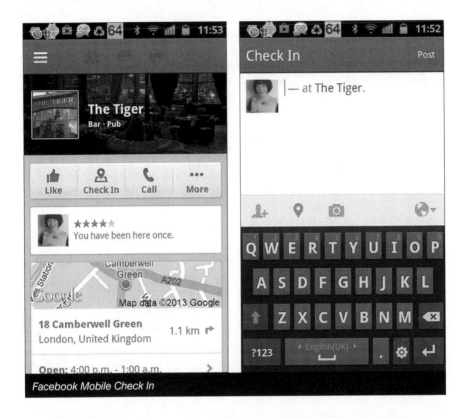

Facebook Mobile Check In

On Facebook local business pages, Facebook users are now being invited to star rate and comment on the venue. With more advanced search options coming to Facebook in 2013, users will soon be able to search for star rated restaurants and bars that have been recommended by their friends, colleagues and family.

Facebook Local Business Page with Star Rating Option

What's Facebook not so good for?

You need to achieve high levels of engagement with Facebook fans to ensure that your content is seen on a regular basis. Facebook has an inbuilt computer algorithm that works out how much a fan has interacted with your content. If the fan ignores your content after liking you, Facebook will eventually stop showing every post as they will deem that it's not so important to your 'fan'. This means you have to invest in various engagement strategies on Facebook to ensure your content remains visible to the widest range of people. The best way you can improve your visibility is to post regularly and to make sure you are posting when your fans are most likely to be online. Promotional posts (paid for posts) can also ensure that your important posts are made visible to your fans even days after the original posting date.

Facebook business page owners cannot send personal messages to other Facebook users (unless they are another business, then you can leave a message on their timeline, or send them a private message).

Google+ Local

Back at the end of May 2012, Google merged Google Places with its social media platform Google+ and then gave it an added edge with scores and reviews from Zagat, the US and International consumer-based restaurant review directory. The end result is that Google+ users can now hit the Local button on their personal Google+ home page and find out where to eat or drink in the locality, with expert and local reviews providing the latest comments and rating scores for the venue.

Local restaurant recommendation from Google+ Local

More than any other platform, Google provides the largest number of listed businesses. This superiority in listings stems from the fact that most food and drink businesses want to be found through search and Google has also made a big effort to make sure they are all listed. Entry on Google Places is free and it's also possible to add special offers for your venue without any extra charge. If you want to reach out to your local tribe and wider customer-base online, then Google+ Local is an absolutely essential listing. Google+ Local information is also accessible when you view Google Maps and search for a place along with a key phrase or word such as 'restaurant', 'bar' or 'café'.

According to Google stats, quoted by econsultancy.com/uk in October 2012, 85% of UK mobile users seek local information on their smartphone, and 81% take action using the local content. In addition, a recent study found that 74% of all Google mobile searches have a local intent[14]. The above statistics add up to a major awareness-building opportunity for restaurants, cafés and bars if they optimise their communications on mobile platforms. On smartphones, users can download the Google+ app and use this powerful search tool to look for local places to eat and drink on their mobile. Once your location is set, Google will immediately list all local places according to your selection. You'll have address, phone number, review ratings both from Zagat and customers, opening times, directions and the option to add your own mark with Check-in option and Photo Upload features. Brilliantly, the venue listing will also include links to any reviews on TripAdvisor, FourSquare, UrbanSpoon or any other online directory that has a review of your venue. If a highly prolific Google+ reviewer has written about your venue, this will also be flagged under your listing. Under the More Options menu, you then continue to have an impressive range of functions that allow you to see the venue at street level, share it with friends, search nearby or report any problems with the listing, for example, does it have the wrong information or has it closed down?

The most recent feature added by Google in October 2012 now allows businesses to add a 360 degree photo of their interior to their Google business profile. When your profile has an associated street view and interior view video, it makes it stand out even more on Google searches. This 360 photo option is available when you commission the services of a Google Trusted Photographer. Once the image has passed strict quality controls including face blurring and image checks it can then be published to your business Google Plus Local page. Just search for Google Trusted Photographer and your location on Google to find out more about photographers who provide this service in your local area.

Google+ Local – Restaurant 360 degree Interior View

I believe that Google+ Local can only go from strength to strength as it continues to provide ever richer levels of data about restaurants, bars and cafés to customers. If you haven't already done so, I highly recommend you claim your Google Places profile (www.google.com/places), so you can ensure your data is optimised and correct. A full listing will give you greater visibility on local search listings and map placements. You can also have a look at the visitor statistics associated with your listing which will give you an indication as to how many people are finding your business through the site.

What's Google+ Local good for?

Whether you're a destination venue or a local business, a full and accurate listing on Google+ Local will ensure your business is visible to fans and casual passers-by alike.

What's Google+ Local not good for?

The Google+ Local interface is all about function over style. It's not the place to make your photographs shine or to tell stories about your brand, but it will provide your customer with all the essentials on your venue.

Instagram

Launched in October 2010, Instagram is an application for mobile phones that allows users to take photos and share them with followers on Instagram itself and across other social media channels such as Facebook. Its main appeal lies in the fact that you can add filters to your photographs and turn them into stunningly beautiful images within a couple of clicks. Fancy making your image look like a Polaroid from the 1970s or a moody black and white still-life? Then Instagram is the perfect medium for you. Unlike other social media platforms, it's entirely free from advertising, which I think is a big part of the reason for its huge success in recent years. However, I doubt this will remain the case for much longer.

Although Instagram is relatively new to the social media world, it's a platform that has had spectacular growth in just the past two years. In a bid to give it some style cache, it was first only made available to iPhone users. However, by 2011, an Android version was launched and then its growth really started to rocket. Between July 2011 and July 2012, the application grew its user base by 17,319%[15]. Even in the extraordinary world of social media, growth figures like this have never been seen previously. Facebook took four years to reach its first 100 million users and Twitter took five years to reach the same mark. By the spring of 2012, Facebook decided to snap up Instagram for a whopping US$1billion. Only time will tell if it's worth the investment, but from my own experience, I've seen that shared Instagram images on Facebook get much higher levels of engagement than practically any other type of content. More generally, photograph posts on Facebook Pages get nearly twice the engagement of any other type of post. I imagine Facebook's head honchos took keen note of this trend and saw Instagram as a veritable content honeypot.

Food and drink photography is a huge trend on Instagram. Users often post pictures of their main courses when both eating out and at home. However, more importantly, Instagram has proved to be a fantastic medium for telling stories and provides a candid view of brands and personalities from behind the scenes. A great example of this is Gennaro

Contaldo's Instagram page at www.instagram.com/gennarocontaldo. Every day he posts updates of what he's up to and who he's with. From his recent travel cookery shows with Antonio Carluccio, he has honed a reputation as a celebrity chef with a devilish sense of humour. On his profile page you'll find everything from rude veg shots, pictures of his fancy new shoe spats or candid-camera shots from his position on stage at a big venue cookery demonstration. His fan base goes wild for his antics and he gets a massive number of shares for his content. He's got that magic combination of a great personality married with fantastic quality content.

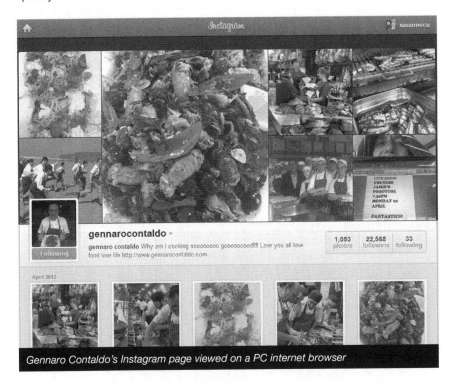

Gennaro Contaldo's Instagram page viewed on a PC internet browser

Instagram Mobile App – Food photo from Gennaro Contaldo's Instagram account

What can you do on Instagram?

Instagram is fast becoming the hot platform for foodies, top chefs and for restaurants and cafes that have an appeal with the younger demographic. The new Instagram profiles that are now accessible online from your PC, laptop or tablet, allow anyone to have a look at Instagram photos from your latest gallery. The top section of the profile page shows a checkerboard selection of your most recent photos and further down the page you can view all your pictures in month order. If you have interesting photos, this onscreen arrangement can look incredibly attractive. Stories from each month can also quickly pop out. The mobile version of the application allows you to instantly keep up with photos from the accounts you follow and you can explore and start following new accounts as and when you wish.

What's Instagram good for?

- It's the perfect medium for telling photo stories as its crisp, clean interface allows you just to focus on the pictures first and foremost.

- It's the perfect place to speak to the movers and shakers, influencers and trend spotters.

- It's also a great platform to attract the celebrity followers who will watch your TV show, buy your DVD, chef books and more.

- If you want to go global with your brand, Instagram is also a great space to hang out as it's not so saturated with content that you cannot be found.

What's Instagram not good for?

- It's not the platform to use for offers or discounts. Style, story-telling, interaction and sharing are the defining features of this channel.

- This channel is definitely one for the younger celebrity-watching demographic or the older hipsters and media peeps. However, this demographic is likely to widen in the near future now that some big brand names are starting to use it as a photo competition channel.

YouTube

YouTube was founded back in February 2005, and the following year it was purchased by Google in its bid to harness the huge draw of video content online. YouTube is one of the social media big hitters, but it is quite different to the other channels in that it receives a lot less interaction. Many people will use YouTube without ever signing up to become a member. Having said that, it still gets the attention of huge numbers of the planet's Internet audience with over 800 million unique visitors using the site each month.

The popularity of this site has not been lost on the hospitality industry and it's becoming more and more common to see restaurants and bars upload videos that give customers a better view of their venue and facilities. Hospitality brands who have deeper pockets have also used YouTube to promote cooking demonstrations and customer testimonials.

Ping Pong's Lychee & Roses Martini demonstration video on YouTube

What's YouTube good for?

- YouTube clips are great for older customers who may want more reassurance before visiting a new destination.

- Women are also more likely to want to research a restaurant before visiting and they appreciate the chance to review more details about the venue before making a decision.

- Travellers or tourists who are planning an important meal out in advance will find video coverage very reassuring.

- As not so many restaurants make use of this marketing channel, it offers you a chance to stand out way and above your competition.

- Video content on YouTube has a very long shelf life and can be viewed by your audience years later and still have an impact.

- YouTube videos play back well on SmartPhones and provide an easier to digest format for the small screen.

What's YouTube not good for?

If you've got a very limited budget, it may be harder to use this channel to best effect. Video content will come across best on YouTube if it's relaxed and conversational, but it still needs a degree of skill applied during production in order to get it right. If you can avail of the skills of a gifted video student you might still be able to create video content that stands out. But in most situations, you will need to invest in the skills of a professional video producer to get the best from your video content.

FourSquare

The FourSquare mobile application and website was initially designed to allow users to check in on their mobile phone at a listed venue, leave tips or comments and earn badges or rewards. This strategy has proved to have had only limited appeal with very low levels of check-ins in comparison to other platforms such as Facebook. However, in order to keep in the market, the company is now much more focused on pushing their Explore, Lists and Offers functions that allow users to tap into the latest information, maps and reviews or tips on bars, restaurants and other food and drink venues in the local area. The strategy is being backed with the opening of a UK office for the FourSquare team. Now they've got representation on our local turf, I expect this platform will develop much more traction in the UK in the near future.

Personalised Recommendations and Explore Suggestions on FourSquare (Website Version)

At time of writing (January 2013), the application has been downloaded by over 25 million users worldwide, and 42% of users login to the application at least once a month. It's currently registering 5 million check-ins a day and is affiliated with over 1 million registered businesses. I know these figures don't seem significant when compared to the big social media behemoths such as Facebook and Twitter. But the trends indicate that specialist platforms will do much better in the future as more people turn from the generic, ad-ridden environment of the biggest players.

How does FourSquare work?

Once you allow the application to track your location, the Explore screen will immediately bring up a list of local venues that have previously been checked-in at by other FourSquare users. More food options nearby, recently opened venues and more places you haven't tried and popular places are also listed in an easy-to-use scrolling window. Every entry will show the latest comment it has received from a FourSquare user. This extra layer of information immediately gives you an impression of the venue from the customer's perspective. If you're interested to see how many places are immediately local to you in one quick view, you can switch to map view which is dotted with interactive pins that provide more information when touched or selected.

The list option allows users to recommend their favourite venues, for example in a locality or according to a type of offer or dish. Sunday roast lists are very popular for example. These lists provide an additional depth of information that allows those new to the area to quickly find the hot venues to visit.

Example of a FourSquare list

When FourSquare started, they became famous for the offers they would provide visitors in exchange for Check-ins. For example, the person who checks in the most within a week or month period, would win the title of 'Mayor' and, if the business decided to set a reward for the Mayor, he or she would be entitled to a special loyalty reward. FourSquare's Swarm feature enables the venue to offer something special when several people all check in at once. These features are still present and can work if they're supported with some marketing collateral in-house. In the near future, FourSquare are also planning to enable local and larger businesses to make offers to people who are exploring on the mobile version of the application. Early adopters of this feature have included American Express who have partnered with brands like Starbucks to offer a credit to the customer's credit card when the customer makes a minimum spend on their Amex card at a venue.

What's FourSquare good for?

- FourSquare is particularly good for giving quality customer feedback on bars and restaurants in a dedicated and easy-to-use mobile application.

- It's a great way for customers to be introduced to new businesses that are in their locality.

- It makes it easier to see what venues are similar in customer appeal to other venues.

- A particular beneficial point is that FourSquare has got a much stronger 'call to action' for customers with the special offers feature it provides.

What's FourSquare not good for?

If an offer is too technical and needs any explanation to the customer you could end up scoring an own goal by providing an attractive looking offer that proves difficult to redeem. It's really important to test drive any offers that you set up with big partners in advance to ensure the mechanics are easy to manage for front of house staff and customers alike.

Pinterest

Pinterest is another recent newcomer to the social media universe. It works as a virtual pinboard website, allowing account holders to 'pin' images from other websites and add them to a personal online pinboard. Pinterest Boards can be set up for just about any topic you care to name. Pinterest has made this collection process really easy for the user by allowing anyone to add a 'pin it' button to the top bar of their web browser. The button only takes a few minutes to install. Hereinafter, the user hits the 'pin it' button any time they see an image they want to add to their Pinterest Board. This action opens a window which lists all the images on the current page and then it's simply up to the user to decide what images they would like to capture through a quick selection process. Once an image has been added to a board, the Pinterest community can then comment on the image or even pin it to one of their own boards. When it works well an interesting image will be shared virally and end up being viewed by hundreds of thousands of people.

Pinterest has become a roaring success with women in the 18 to 35 year old demographic and currently has about 48.7 million users (ComScore and Reuters). We know about 60% of those are USA based, with the rest of the audience spread across the world. Unlike Instagram which thrives on sharing photos that tell stories and that show the personality of a brand or celebrity, Pinterest is more often about the aspirational, the trendy, the stylishly shot photograph. If the images don't major on one of those attractor points, then humour or cuteness can also generate engagement.

According to Repinly.com, pins about Food and Drink make up 11.6% of all pins, making it the single most popular individual category ahead of DIY & Crafts, Home Décor, Women's Fashion and Hair & Beauty. Having said that, food and drink coverage seems to gravitate towards the following sub-sectors on Pinterest, including gourmet cuisine, home baking, cupcakes, occasion cooking and cocktails for weddings and parties. If these categories are meaningful to your business, or your ideal customer is a female aged 18 to 35, then Pinterest is definitely worth a much closer look.

Images of Duck Soup Soho on Pinterest.com

What's Pinterest good for?

- It's a great platform if you want to interact with women in the 18–35 year old age group and male and female design & innovation fans.

- Fine dining destinations, businesses specialising in baking & cakes, wedding caterers or venues, venues for special events, niche food products for sale online can all benefit from investing time and effort on Pinterest.

- Some data is now indicating that high-spending, younger females in the UK are particularly keen on Pinterest. If your brand is high-fashion in any sense, it's highly recommended you hotfoot it on to Pinterest asap.

What's Pinterest not good for?

It's still a niche market platform in the UK, so don't waste your time on Pinterest if you don't have high quality brand or design-led content to share.

++++++

Knowing what social media channels to use is one thing. Making effective use of your time on these channels is quite another. In the next chapter, I'll give you guidance on a number of social media publishing tools which you and your team can use to save time and schedule ahead. I'll also provide you with an overview of the other key software tools you need to invest in, for improved in-house digital marketing management.

CHAPTER 8

Your Essential Digital Marketing Tools

The Changing World of Software

Today, with the aid of the latest digital marketing tools, it's now possible to turn your humble laptop or desktop pc into a super-charged marketing machine. Whatever it is you want to do, whether you want to collect customer details online, send out designer-standard email newsletters, profile your social media followers or get stats from your website visitors, you now have the option to manage all these tasks for an incredibly affordable monthly fee. Gone are the days when you needed to buy your software on CD and load it onto every computer used by marketing in your office. Forget about fees for software upgrades every couple of years. Now, the latest Internet-based software solutions let you log in from any computer, anytime, anywhere and save the files you're working on securely online. Upgrades are part-and-parcel of the monthly fee and the majority of these online software providers roll out new improvements every couple of months. I find it amazing to think that most of these products were just in their infancy or not in existence at all only five years ago.

I believe this online software revolution is going to radically change the way you market your business, if it hasn't already started to do so. These solutions are cheaper, more powerful and provide you with better data security than you ever previously had. For example, in the past if you'd had a fire or a computer theft at your premise, all your data could have been lost in a puff. Now, your files are instantly backed up online, and are mirrored on another bank of servers for even further security by these new online software providers. Many of their server farms are high security, terrorist and weather proof spaces. Could you say the same thing about your local office computer servers?

In my role as a digital marketing consultant, I regularly provide advice on the latest software marketing tools. In this chapter, I'm going to introduce you to some of the essential tools I currently recommend to hospitality businesses.

Customer Relationship Management Solutions

Top of the list, I recommend that you invest in a Customer Relationship Management solution, or CRM system as they are usually known, in order to start collecting and managing your customer data in a smarter, more cost-efficient way.

Typically, most good online CRM systems will offer you the following features;

- Online customer data storage

- Customer data capture forms for your website and Facebook

- Email newsletter templates and email delivery options

- Customer data labelling or grouping

- Special Offer coupon creation and management (for PC and Mobile)

- Loyalty card management

- Customer response analytics

- Facebook Special Offer setup

- Social Media follower analytics

Prices for a basic restaurant CRM system can start from as little as GB£99 for a single venue per month. There are also systems on the market such as Livebookings.co.uk that take integration to the ultimate step and include online reservations. You'll be charged a bit more for this service, but I believe this added integration gives you even more control over your business marketing.

If you are a business that still stores all your customer information on a spreadsheet and you're not sure if the above features are worth GB£99+ a month, then please, listen up! That spreadsheet is costing you time and money to just keep it up-to-date.

1. Your spreadsheet is probably full of data errors. For example, a spreadsheet won't tell you if a customer has stopped using his email address. If you are not using a CRM or Email Newsletter tool, the only way you can check dead email addresses is to sort through the bounce backs that are sent back to your email inbox. These emails are also full of technical code and it can be difficult for the non-technical person to work out the precise reason for the bounceback.

2. If a customer is not happy receiving emails from you, she'll have to email you directly and ask to be unsubscribed from your list. You're legally obliged to remove unhappy subscribers from your list, so this is another task you can't avoid.

3. If you want to send emails to smaller groups from your list, then there will be more time spent sorting and separating names each time you want to do a mailing from your spreadsheet.

4. How many people opened your last email? How many clicked on the links and which links did they click on? None of this data is available to you in your spreadsheet.

Please believe me, I could go on, but spreadsheets are time consuming, prone to error and difficult to get meaningful data out of. This is unless you happen to be a spreadsheet report-building whizzkid, which I guess most people are not.

A CRM system on the other hand is going to offer your business multiple benefits without the blood, sweat and tears of a spreadsheet.

- Customers can add their data directly to your database via your website form or Facebook page app

- Your business can send personalised marketing emails with or without redeemable coupons

- You can see how many people have read your emails and used your coupons in a couple of clicks

- Without being a designer, it's possible to create attractive email designs by using pre-designed templates

- Manage smaller email lists for targeted groups of customers

- Share offers and newsletter updates with your social media followers

- Enable customers to unsubscribe, freeing up admin time on your side

When you think about the hours you'll save and the additional revenue you could generate, you'll start to realise how this approach wins hands down over keeping your data locked up in a simple, but not very versatile spreadsheet.

There are several CRM systems on the market that offer the above functionality with various other bells and whistles. Whatever system you select, the main thing is to make sure it supports all the tasks you've outlined in your Marketing Plan. As technology improvements are on-going, I also recommend that you review your system once every two years, to make sure it's still the best solution for your business.

Social Media Management

Next up, you can save plenty of time for you and your team if you invest in a Social Media Management software solution. The main benefit offered by these solutions is that they enable you to keep track of and manage all your social media communications in one place. The big name providers include Hootsuite and SproutSocial, and there are plenty of wily competitors chomping at their heels with even more powerful new analytic features. To make sure you find the best solution, it's a good idea to check the latest reviews when you decide to set up for the first time or change your account from another provider.

Most of the better social media management software products will enable you to:

- Enter your update and then send it to all your social media channels

- Schedule your updates for future times and dates

- Set up filters to keep watch on mentions of your brand name, your hashtags or keywords you want to follow

- Find and track your most influential followers

- Research and follow other Twitter accounts

- Track views, clicks, reTweets and shares generated by your social media content

- Integrate your social media statistics with your website analytics so you can see how much website traffic you are gaining from Twitter, Facebook etc.

- Setup multiple administrators and provide different permission levels dependent on position

Some more advanced CRM systems are also building these social media management features into their solutions, so if you want a completely all-in-one solution ask the sales representative if they are included or can be added on. Generally the cheaper route is to use one of the above stand-alone systems which are on offer for as little as US$10 per month for a standard professional account. Some providers will even offer their software for free if you only want to manage up to five social media accounts with access to the basic features.

The more integrated your marketing software is, the more powerful it is, as it can extract and analyse data from your email list, social media and loyalty card holders. But this integration usually comes at a cost, so you'll have to weigh that up against the value you are able to extract from the system. The more data you collect, the more important it is to have someone in your organisation who can actively review and extract insights from the data for your business benefit. This is what the smartest businesses do, so I strongly recommend you make an effort to get data-wise in order to become more responsive to your customer's behaviour and communication. Integrated systems are also easier for your marketing manager to use, as they don't have to swap in and out of different systems over the course of the day. Over time, that time wasted moving from one system to another all adds up. If you're a larger organisation who can afford to pay a professionally trained marketer to do the job, then the time saving could be worth the move to a completely integrated system.

Email Newsletter Management

In an ideal world, I would recommend that you use your CRM system as your main email newsletter management tool. When you manage promotions, emails and social media all through the one dashboard, you have an integrated view of your customer data and you're not wasting time trying to take data from one system and marry it with data from another. This makes it easier for you to make smart, quick decisions which I think is one of the biggest benefits of these integrated systems.

However, if your marketing spend is a real concern, you can manage your email marketing list using a standalone Email Newsletter Management provider such as http://mailchimp.com/,

www.constantcontact.com/uk/index.jsp or www.aweber.com/ .
These affordable online solutions will enable you to:

- Send personalised emails to your newsletter subscribers

- Customise your email design using one of the pre-designed templates

- Monitor open rates, click through rates and shares

- Allow customers to subscribe to your list via your website or Facebook

- Allow customers to unsubscribe online

- Manage lists for different groups of customers

- Quickly identify bounce back emails

Your existing spreadsheet of contacts can also be quickly imported into the software as an Excel or a CSV file, so you literally can be up and running with a new marketing email within half a day (dependent on your in-house team skill level).

Online Surveys

One of the oldest and best ways to improve your business is to regularly ask for feedback from your customers. The old-fashioned way would be to question people in person and fill in the details on paper questionnaires. Now we've got tablet computers and easy-build online survey software, you can quickly collect this data at tasting events and more casually with one-to-one chats during the normal course of business. I helped Towercrest set up a customer feedback survey when I first started working for them in the summer of 2011. I wrote a questionnaire and then created an online form version of the survey using a GoogleDocs survey template that's provided free with any GoogleApps business account. Our marketing co-ordinator Jo then spent time in venue approaching customers and asked if they would spare a few minutes to answer the form question in exchange for a free drink.

This first survey brought up some fantastic feedback that helped us to make immediate, positive changes within the venue. For example, we had been having trouble getting customers to go and take table space upstairs, so we were interested to find out why it was such an issue. It turned out that most of the customers interviewed did not even realise that they could go and eat upstairs. This issue was quickly rectified with proactive communication on the floor with customers who were looking for somewhere to sit and we also installed much more prominent signage to make it clearer that there was additional seating upstairs. Before the survey the team could have argued amongst themselves as to what was the issue. Hard data made it much clearer what the issue was and gave us a mandate to make quick and effective changes. With a little help from your web developer, you can also set up an online survey to pop up when customers visit your website. Whatever customer issues you're trying to come to grips with, why not try running a survey for yourself? You might be surprised and enlightened by the results.

Social Media Auto Response

There are some additional features that are not available within the social media management packages I mentioned previously that can help you to be even more responsive to new Twitter followers. Online services such as www.SocialOomph.com enable you to set up your Twitter account so that you will automatically follow anyone who follows you. It also allows you to set up systems where you can add an approval level before a Twitter account can become one of your followers. This is especially good practice if you want to weed out follows from people who are just following you in order to get your attention. Unfortunately there are businesses who have no idea how to use the medium properly and who just want to shout about their product or services. If your account ends up attracting lots of these spammer tweeters, you can usually set them hopping by activating this approval process. It's one hoop too many for Twitter users who are just looking for a quick win. Another attractive feature offered by SocialOomph is the ability to send a Twitter direct message to anyone who follows you. Within this message you can immediately thank them for the follow and perhaps promote a special offer as an incentive to visit. These features are available for about US$8 per month, so again, you've got the option to improve the way you reach out to new followers with a very small additional investment.

Design Software

Once you've commissioned some attractive templates from your friendly designer for your menu and in-venue posters, it should be possible to get your in-house team to make amendments to weekly specials menus, email newsletter images, monthly toilet door posters, Facebook promotions and more. All you'll need is a design software package that allows you to make text or image amendments which can then be saved out as a high resolution PDF file for an external printer, as a PNG file for on-screen use, or can be printed straight out to your in-house colour printer. Ask your designer if she can provide you with a template that works in the software package you're using in-house. Designers tend to use the most expensive software such as Adobe Photoshop or Illustrator, or Adobe InDesign for print. To buy all these packages can cost you thousands of pounds up front or from about GB£17.50 per month if you sign up for the basic online version at www.adobe.com.

However, why not ask your designer to export an image background or components that can then be setup for use in a cheaper design software such as Microsoft Office Publisher (which you can buy as single license as an add-on to Microsoft Office for about UK£99 (UK only). Whoever uses the software in-house will need to have some basic design skills, but they certainly don't need to be a fully trained designer. I've worked with several marketing managers who are more than capable of adapting and reusing existing templates for new promotions. If money is really limited, you can work with Microsoft PowerPoint to create and save files for print and screen. However, I would recommend a package like Publisher as it gives you a lot more control and offers a fantastic range of readymade templates that you can adapt for your own purposes if you can't afford a full-time or part-time designer.

Blogs

If you're looking to attract a 'foodie' audience, you may want to invest in a blog for your website, where you share stories about your food and drink and where you showcase your latest creations with fantastic photographs. Blogs are great for connecting with your tribe as they allow people to comment on your blog posts and visitors can also chat in the comments section with other people who have commented as well as with the author of the blog. You can set up your blog using websites such as Wordpress.com, Blogger.com or Tumblr.com if you want to create a more visually led blog. The website can either sit on the blog provider's domain (e.g. www.mychefblog.wordpress.com) or it can be integrated into your own website with the help of a web developer or a more technically proficient marketer.

Dependent on your views about interaction, you can make the blog open for comments, or switch off this facility. If you do leave the comments area open, make sure to check for spammers who often leave comments on blogs in order to advertise other third parties. There are solutions to help you deal with spammers. It's probably best to speak to your web developer to find out what the latest solution is for dealing with this when you set up your blog online. For example, you could ask for a CAPTCHA solution which asks the contributor to type in a code to verify that they are a human being before proceeding.

Website Solutions

Yes, even websites for restaurants and bars can now be set up to go in a matter of days or even hours if you're very organised and have all your content ready to upload. From as little as US$10 a month you can set up an account using services such as www.letseat.at and create a website that integrates with online reservation services such as www.OpenTable.co.uk and email newsletter software such as www.ConstantContact.com These vendors also allow you to create special offer pages within your Facebook page and you can easily integrate your Twitter feed onto your website pages. The website will immediately be optimised for mobile phones and you can even add videos from your YouTube and Vimeo accounts. For a bit more spend, you can order a customised design that works especially for your brand. I think these vendors offer quite extraordinary value for money and are going to help even the smallest businesses to do a fantastic marketing job online.

As I write, Wordpress, one of the world's most popular blogging websites, has just launched a new website template especially for restaurants. Now for a ridiculously small amount of money per year, you can set up a restaurant website that includes all the basics you might want from a site including sections about you, reservation information, a map and a list of the latest things on your menu. It looks so simple and stylish, I imagine a lot of start-up or cash-strapped restaurants are going to find this a very cheap and cheerful way to get up and running online. And because the template is offered by Wordpress, there is an integrated blog as part of the package. Really, when I see all these incredible new services I worry for web designers. Why should businesses pay several hundred or even several thousand pounds on a website when you can now setup in a flash with so much sophisticated functionality included?

Analytics

Finally, as with all other aspects of business, you need to keep track of your online marketing performance. Most of the online tools featured above include an analytics area where you can check out the performance of your online content.

When it comes to tracking your website performance, Google Analytics is one of the best tools out there. And wonderfully, it is completely free. The only cost, if you're not able to do this yourself, is to get some assistance putting some google HTML code into your website footer which forms part of each page on your website. Once this code is placed in each of your website page files it will immediately start sending back information to your Google Analytics account. You'll be able to see how many people visited your site, how often they visit, what country and town they come from, what content they looked at and how long they spent on the site. If you want more detail, you can track the path that visitors have typically taken through your website, for example, what page did they start on, where did they go next, how many pages deep did they go before leaving? If you want to check how many people have been reviewing your Christmas menu package, you simply go to the Content tab and select Overview to see how many visits this section of your website has had. As you make improvements to your content, you can check your analytics panel to see what changes have encouraged more visitors or where you might still need to do more work.

Social Media analytics within Google Analytics, Facebook or Hootsuite will show you which posts are your most popular and what levels of engagement you generated from each post. For example, you can see if Facebook or Twitter users commented on or shared the content and how many people actually clicked on the links within the posts. All this information should be reviewed regularly to ensure that you are going in the right direction. On Facebook, you'll also see figures regarding your reach. This number indicates how many friends of friends have seen your updates, comments and posts whilst browsing Facebook on their PC or mobile. As you start to get more sophisticated with your social media usage, you'll want to track the usage and reach of Twitter #hashtags you have created to encourage social media chat about a particular campaign or subject you want to be associated with.

Successful social media influencers are now being scored and graded by social media influence measurement websites such as www. peerindex.com and klout.com. The score is typically made of three components. You'll score a certain amount of points for the number of followers you have. If there is a large ratio difference between the number of people who follow you and the number of people you follow, which indicates that far more people follow you, then this will bump up your score further. The number of people who engage with you and share or comment on your content will also affect your score. If you are followed by a large number of influential social media users, this will raise your score further still. So for example, the British lovey and arch-gadget geek Stephen Fry is highly active on Twitter and has a Klout score of 90 out of 100. Rude food lover and worldwide famous chef Jamie Oliver is not far behind with a score of 85. And his cheeky Italian mentor Gennaro Contaldo has a Klout score of 59. Many online marketing tools are now including these scores so you can see how influential your fans and followers are. This is ultra-important information when it comes to identifying and seeking out those social media savvy customers who are also loyal or budding tribe members.

Each of the tools I have mentioned in this chapter probably warrant a whole book in their own right. To get a more specific marketing tool recommendation for your business, I recommend you speak to a marketing consultant or you spend more time researching the latest options and reviews online on leading marketing news websites such as http://www.mashable.com and www.socialmediaexaminer.com.

CHAPTER 9

Getting Results

As some of the top business brains say, you can have the best strategy in the world, but it is not worth the paper it's written on if you don't know how to deliver. The last thing I want is for you to read this book and then to end up thinking, but how do I actually make this happen? This, my friend, is where your inner project manager needs to grind into action. Every project, regardless of what it sets out to do, will benefit from a step-by-step project management plan and tactics. In this chapter I will walk you through my tried-and-tested route for getting the job done.

Communication Essentials

Regardless of what you do in business, it's essential you look at how your team communicates first. If the people in your business have trouble communicating with each other, I can guarantee you that you'll have trouble implementing any kind of change. I could probably write a whole book on this one topic, but as you no doubt want to cut to the chase, here's a double quick guide to improving the quality of communications in your business.

Regular Team Communications

Set regular team meeting slots throughout the week or month. When your team know there is a regular dedicated time to discuss issues, they can prepare any questions or communications they need to share in advance. If you only run impromtu meetings or irregular meetings, or worse still, no team meetings at all, this sends out a big fat sign that people's opinions or concerns are not that important. I believe this is one of the biggest motivation killers in business.

Communications Ground Rules

When you get together for a one-to-one or group meeting, there are some basic ground rules that everyone should be aware of:

Be on Time

Lateness should not be tolerated as it shows disrespect for other people's time. Make a real effort to have meetings start and finish on time.

Listen

Always show other people respect by listening to what they have to say. If anyone in your group has a habit of talking too much, you can set a ground rule that people have up to 1 or 2 minutes to make their point. This tactic generally helps keep people on track.

Chair

Have a chair, someone who's responsible for keeping the meeting agenda on track and for curtailing people who want to speak for too long or who go off topic.

Meetings are for Making Decisions and Learning

When you set a meeting, decide an agenda in advance. Ask the attendees if they would like to add anything to the agenda. Make sure the agenda is ordered so that the most important items are dealt with first.

At the meeting, most of your time should be spent making decisions. Keep reports to a minimum. Instead, use most of the time to constructively solve problems as a group. One of the great benefits of this approach is that it enables group learning. If one manager brings an issue to the table and another manager comes up with a solution, everyone else at the table can learn from that conversation. When you come together regularly to solve problems, you can radically accelerate your organisation's learning potential.

Keep reports

Make someone responsible for keeping notes at meetings. Most importantly, include agreed actions, who is responsible and agreed completion dates for each point. Then distribute these notes to all attendees after the meeting.

Flag the Important Stuff, Ditch the Trivia

Email overload has become one of the top scourges of modern working life. Make sure to keep emails to a minimum. Always ask yourself who really needs to read this email before copying it to everyone in the organisation. I suggest using a Prefix code on your internal business email titles, to help people immediately see what's important and what is for your reference only.

- ASAP – I need you to make a decision on this today

- DEC – I need you to make a decision on this within 48 hours

- REP – I'm reporting back

- FYI – thought you'd like to know about this

If you are having a face-to-face conversation, let people know at the start if it's important or not, e.g. 'I just need a few minutes of your time to help me make a decision on this.' Rather than starting with a big pre-amble about the story behind the request. With people under so much pressure to perform these days, we can really help each other out by being respectful of other's time, especially when people are busy or stressed over other issues.

Establish your Priorities

In a perfect world we'd be able to go all guns blazing on all our objectives from day one. In practice though, this notion is completely impractical. If you start to load several new plans on your team in one go, I can guarantee that the resulting output is going to be totally dismal. Most people end up running around like headless chickens if they are asked to push through on several initiatives at once.   My first recommendation is that you phase the delivery of different objectives over time. And in order to do this, you first need to get clear about your priorities.

What are the important things that you want to achieve within the business? You will have already set out several objectives for the year in your marketing plan. Now, you need to decide which objectives are the most important and which ones need to be worked on first.

Here's a simple model that can help you to identify the jobs to prioritise going forward.

Priority Setting. With thanks to Endpoint for this example of Priority Setting chart

An objective will be plotted higher or lower on the chart, dependent on how much positive impact it will have for your business. From left to right, you can position your objectives dependent on how difficult or easy they may be to implement. Once all your key objectives are plotted, it will then be easier to see what objectives are high or medium priority, and where you can find your quick wins. It can also help you weed out any objectives that could be difficult to do with a resulting low impact or lower impact in comparison to other objectives.

I believe identifying quick wins is enormously important at the start. The successful implementation of some initial quick wins is great for morale and helps get the whole team behind a new plan. Quick wins are also a brilliant way to get momentum going. There is nothing harder than to try and push a big boulder that is standing stock still in the middle of the road. However, once a boulder starts moving it's going to take a lot less effort to keep it going. Remember, momentum is your friend. Do everything you can to keep the energy of your plan going from day one.

Once the quick wins have helped to get you up and running, you can now turn your attention to the big impact, but more difficult priorities. It has always helped when I look at a big audacious plan as just a series of a thousand little steps. Each little step in itself is not so intimidating. Eventually over time, you'll look back at the culmination of all these small movements and realise you've made a huge journey. And so it is with the big and difficult priorities. Within the delivery of this one objective, there will also be tasks that are high or low impact, easy or difficult. First, write down all the tasks that will need to be completed in order to realise this particular objective. For example, you may have set an objective to start measuring your marketing results against your target goals. If you've not done this before, it might seem like a difficult task, but with a methodical step-by-step approach, you can start to identify what you can do quickly and what you might need assistance with.

For example, in order to start measuring results you'll need to implement the following tasks:

- Establish which results you want to measure

- Create your target numbers for each marketing activity

- Create a spreadsheet to store your measurements

- Identify what tools you will use to gather your statistics

- Decide when you will create and present a results report (e.g. every week, every month, or every quarter)

If you know you need to do something, but you're still not sure how to go about it, then this task will need to be preceded with a research task or a delegation task. For example, if you don't know what results you want to measure, you can add a task to find an expert who can help you answer that question. Eventually, you end up with a list of completely achievable tasks. More importantly, you've overcome the big mental block of looking at a big objective and not knowing where to start.

The 10 Day Rule

I recommend no single task should take more than 10 working days to complete. If you think it will take more than that, it should be broken down into two or more smaller tasks. From my days in software development, I came across a project management technique called 'The Sprint'. A Sprint is typically a 10 day period where a team will work on a particular task or inter-related group of smaller tasks. Why 10 days you ask? Some software project managers found that if they gave a developer a task to complete in 10 days, he was more likely to successfully complete the job. It seems that the human mind responds much better to goals that are set for the near future. A week was seen as too little time. If the schedule was set over a month, the developer had a lower sense of urgency which resulted in poorer time planning over the period. In the end they found that 10 days provided the developers with the optimum sense of urgency and comfort.

To reiterate, in each Sprint two week period, you may have several people working on different tasks at the same time, but they all have a part to play in the overall plan. Another element of the Sprint is that the tasks are given an order and are allocated before the Sprint period starts. Once the Sprint starts, the developer is not asked to take on any new projects or tasks until the 10 day period is complete. This task lock-down approach gives the developer more assurance that he will not be thrown any needless distractions. Ultimately people work best when they feel like they have more control over their work load.

Keep the Momentum Going

When you lose momentum, there's a big risk that your project will grind to a halt and fail to start again. Worse still, you've wasted all that initial energy that went into starting the project in the first place. An important mechanism that helps the Sprint team to keep the momentum going and remain productive is a 15 minute daily 'scrum' meeting. Everyone gathers in a circle and the meeting is held standing up so as not to encourage people to spend too much time talking. The key aim here is to keep momentum going and to nip issues in the bud as soon as they crop up. A 'Scrum Master' or group leader will ask everyone in turn:

- What did you achieve yesterday?

- What are you planning to do today?

- Is there anything blocking you from doing what you need to do today?

Any issues that come up in the meeting can be answered on the spot if they only need a short comment from the team leader or manager to get things back on track. If it takes more than a minute to solve the issue then the manager should follow up on that conversation with the individual after the scrum.

Granted, the restaurant environment is a far cry from the software developer's world. However, I believe these techniques are transferrable to a wide range of scenarios. With ever increasing rises in stock and labour costs, the one place we can claw back a lead is through smarter project management strategies. Only this morning, as I was writing this chapter, I was interrupted with a call from my brother David. His wife, Miriam is a senior manager in the Irish Health Service and David told me how she's currently involved in rolling out a new LEAN project management process. The Sprint team technique is one that is commonly used by LEAN (rapid prototyping) or AGILE-trained project managers. He was so interested in what he heard from her that he started to think about how he could apply these project management techniques to his own tomato growing business.

If I was to pick an example of how your business could use the Sprint approach, I would suggest trying it out on an event or seasonal campaign. The run up to Christmas, for example, is an incredibly busy time. There are hundreds of small and large tasks that will contribute to making your festive campaign a success. At the very start, list out all the tasks you will need to allocate to the team between the start and completion. Then group the tasks in order of priority. I suggest you plan several Sprint periods from the summer onwards. For each Sprint, you will allocate only the tasks you need to prioritise for that period. You might start with a creative campaign development Sprint in July. Simultaneously your executive chef will be developing the Christmas menu as you'll want to mail out your Christmas menu to the corporate customers by email in the first week of September. Have at least a few scrum meetings with your project team each week to make sure everyone is on track. I think it's also helpful to have people from different departments at the same scrum meeting, as everyone is better able to see the part that they and others play in the bigger vision. This can be a big motivating factor when you are trying to achieve a complex task.

Remember, I'm not suggesting you tie up lots of time with this process. It should take no more than 15 minutes maximum. Anything more than this and it starts to become counterproductive. Also, remember to run meetings standing up as this keeps the pace going.

People and Resource Management

Before you start the Sprint phase, you'll also need to go through your master task list and work out who's going to do each job and what extra resources they may need to complete the task. You should also consider are they fully fit for the job, do they have the right skill set, or will they need some coaching or education before they can get on with the job?

Briefing your Team

Once you've established who's doing what and if they need any extra support, you can move on to the briefing. Dependent on the complexity of the task, very simple tasks can be briefed in a group situation and more complex tasks should be briefed one-to-one. The success of the outcome is often highly dependent on a clearly structured brief, so I recommend you take the time to work through the following procedure.

When briefing a task:

- Explain why the task is being delegated to that person or people.

- Explain why it is important to the business and how it fits into the bigger scheme.

- State the required results. Let the person know what successful completion will look like. Outline any targets or measurements of success for the task.

- Agree what resources are required to do the job. The person who is doing the job may have another perspective on what's required, so make sure to hear them out on this point.

- Agree deadlines. Is there a target completion date? If it's an on-going task, set a review date. If there are several parts to the task, what are the priorities?

- Explain how you will do any checks during the progress of the job. If you don't explain this in advance, you can come across as interfering or that you don't trust the person to do the job.

- Ask the person to reiterate the brief in their own words and to ask any questions before you complete. This is an importance phase as it enables you to more clearly see if the brief has been understood. It also enables the person to step into the role and take more ownership.

Finally, consider if anyone else needs to know about this briefing. Who will it impact and ask the briefee to contribute their thoughts on this question. Are there any complicated company politics involved that they need to be aware of? If the task is of importance, you will also need to brief your boss, or other senior managers. Make sure you do the briefing to senior management yourself rather than leaving it the person to brief their seniors on their new responsibility.

Tracking

Stick to what you agreed in the briefing regarding tracking progress or performing any quality control measures. As recommended above, you can use regular Scrum meetings for a progress update from the whole team.

Review

In the closing phases of the task, review progress and provide feedback. If the task has been successful make sure to let people know that they have done a good job. Everyone appreciates a little clap on the back for a job well done. If a task has not been successfully completed, review the issues and consider what lessons have been learnt. It's excellent practice to review the final stage of a Sprint with the whole group, so any lessons learned can be shared with everyone. Remember also to review the performance measurements you set out to track. Real data will always bring a much needed pinch of realism to the review phase.

Tackling Your Blocks

Applying all of the above processes and tactics can make a huge difference to the outcome of your plans. However, I know from hard experience that people still have the habit of coming up with a whole range of reasons for not getting the job done. Let's look at some of the more common excuses and see what can be done to overcome them.

We Don't Have Enough Time

I believe a lack of time is commonly symptomatic of a lack of planning and priority setting. In order to become a master of the effective use of your time, you need to learn and appreciate the need for planning and doing the important things first. Planned projects are proved to have a much better chance of success. Good priority setting will ensure that you don't waste time on the tasks that have low impact. When you plan, you also take the time to look at what's coming up the road and you are in a better position to prepare for change.

At a deeper psychological level, the lack of time excuse can also be symptomatic of a fear of change or an inability to deal with change. If you find yourself stuck in a certain pattern of behaviour where you keep yourself perpetually busy in order to avoid dealing with certain issues in your life, then you'd be well advised to explore the causes. Examining past events that have led you to act out in this way, can help you to overcome these behaviours and take on new, more productive habits. For example, when a person is perpetually stuck in fire-fighting mode he has usually convinced himself that the work can't be done in a less stressful way. He may have grown up in an environment where this sort of behaviour is the norm. He probably finds himself attracted to working for businesses that also work this way. Or if he owns the business he ends up unwittingly re-creating this culture. He might not realise this consciously but even though it's difficult to bear, the scenario is familiar so he feels like this is a place where he can fit in.

On the other hand, some people will have mastered the art of being busy but not necessarily productive. 'If I just work hard and focus on getting as many things done as possible', she says, 'my job will be safe and I won't need to worry'. Both of these characters don't take the time out to consider if they are actually working on the smart stuff. They keep busy doing stuff that's always been done. As my old friends Surekha and Gerry reminded me last night, if you keep doing the same old, same old, don't be surprised if you get the same old, same old! So be brave. Take time to ask yourself are there any underlying issues that are playing out here. A frank examination of your behaviour could set you on the path to a better way of working. If you find self-examination difficult, a good business / life coach or business mentor can help you to identify issues, reflect on your actions and embrace change.

We Don't Have Enough Money

I sincerely believe that if you invest in gathering a tribe to your business, a lack of money will cease to be a problem. Regular, consistent engagement with your tribe of loyal customers will sustain your finances through good times and bad. You won't need to stump up the money for everything overnight. Go back to the early section of this chapter, work out your priority objectives and look for quick wins that will start to bring you results without costing a fortune. As your cashflow improves, you can then invest in the important projects that will have an even bigger positive impact on your business in the longer term.

It may well be that it's a case of halting spend on less effective activities and moving your budget and resources to areas where the investment will have much more impact. For example, when I started working with Towercrest, their original marketing budget had allocated several thousand pounds on advertising. By the end of the year, they had actually spent no more than a few hundred pounds on advertising. Instead this budget was diverted to more impactful activities such as events, social media and email marketing.

We Don't Have Any Bright Ideas

If you don't feel like you have the right people in place to come up with bright marketing ideas on a regular basis then it is high time you filled this gap. If your marketing manager is low on experience, but is high on ideas and has a good work ethic, then he or she has the potential to learn and develop on the job with the right guidance and management. I'd much prefer to employ this sort of candidate than someone with an arm's length of qualifications who can't come up with a good idea to save their lives. If you're a bigger organisation, structure you team to include a combination of people who will bring different skills and levels of creativity to your business. If your budget is really limited, either find someone who can divide their time between office and marketing duties, or operations support and marketing duties. Then you can use a consultant to help get you on track with the higher level strategy and to assist on any training requirements for your in-house marketing person. If you are a bigger operation, you also have the option to work with a specialist marketing or creative agency whilst keeping the day-to-day marketing communications work in-house.

We Don't Feel Comfortable Asking for Feedback on Social Media

Much as I would like to say, 'oh don't worry about social media, you can save it for some time in the future', I'm afraid that would just be helping you to put off the inevitable. Dining and drinking are two of the most sociable things that we do and as a result they have become completely natural and intertwined bed-fellows with social media. Everyone likes a good restaurant recommendation. As a natural extension of this tendency, your customers are now flocking to the web to get real world feedback on your food, drink and service from social media newsfeeds, restaurant directories and ratings websites. This tendency is not going to stop. In fact it's just going to keep on increasing to the point where customer feedback will become the main yardstick every business measures itself against. Even the much vaunted food and drink critics are going to lose their thunder and their impact. The hype and the glitz of a big advertising budget will have continuously decreasing impact. So get in now, roll your sleeves up and start giving the customer what he or she wants; a continuous and open line of communication.

We're Not Trendy Enough for this Tribe Malarkey

Building a tribe is not about being hip, or techie. It might seem like a trendy, new-fangled strategy, especially the bits that work with social media, but in other ways this is the oldest strategy in the book. It all boils down to creating deeper, more meaningful relationships with your customers. It's not about treating people like automatons or cash cows. It's about seeing customers as individuals who will be delighted at the experience of making a genuine connection with you and your team.

The New Marketing Manifesto for Restaurants, Bars and Cafés

Before you finish, I'd like leave you with a one last parting message. I truly believe we are experiencing revolutionary times in the field of marketing and it feels fitting to write a New Marketing Manifesto for

Restaurants, Cafés and Bars that reflects these seismic changes. I hope it will help you to more easily take away the big messages I've included in this book and to apply them with revolutionary zeal to your next marketing plan.

The New Marketing Manifesto for Restaurants, Bars and Cafés

1. **BUILD A TRIBE NOT A CUSTOMER BASE**
   Learn how to engage with loyal and influential customers, partners and friends. Ditch the sales pitch and seek to build trust instead.

2. **EXPRESS AUTHENTIC VALUES**
   Connect with your customers by sharing your values and beliefs in a credible way.

3. **OPEN THE CONVERSATION**
   Stop broadcasting and start talking to your customers online, on social media channels, in venue and beyond.

4. **PROACTIVE LISTENING & RESPONSE**
   Listen out for online conversations about your business and respond quickly and smartly.

5. **GO MOBILE & SOCIAL IN VENUE AND BEYOND**
   Be found and easy to connect with on mobile. Allow mobile users to interact and follow you at the table or bar via smartphone.

6. **TURN MARKETING INTO A TEAM SPORT**
   Involve the whole team in your marketing initiatives

7. **GET AGILE**
   Become an Agile business with the latest cloud-based software, rapid prototyping processes and quick response marketing initiatives.

8. **JOIN UP THE DOTS TO GET THE BIGGER PICTURE**
   Use the data to get a smarter view of your performance.

9. **GET SMART ABOUT DELIVERY**
   Apply the latest thinking in people and project management for even better results.

A Final Wish

So there you have it. If you follow this manifesto, I believe you will have what it takes to build a tribe full of highly engaged and loyal fans around your business. I wish you well in your venture and your tribe-building and I look forward to hearing how you've taken the ideas in this book and applied them for your business success. What are you waiting for? Your tribe awaits!

REFERENCES

1. http://www.camra.org.uk/article.php?group_id=8988

2. http://www.fpb.org/news/2491/Forum_urges_government_to_tear_up_weak_pub_industry_proposal_following_new_evidence_of_pubco_stitch_up_.htm

3. http://www.bighospitality.co.uk/Trends-Reports/Food-dubbed-lifeline-for-pubs-despite-higher-operating-costs

4. http://www.bighospitality.co.uk/Business/Rising-cost-of-food-is-biggest-concern-for-restaurant-operators

5. http://www.bighospitality.co.uk/Trends-Reports/Hospitality-operators-warned-to-prepare-for-food-inflation-surge-in-2013

6. http://aaronallen.com/blog/restaurant-marketing/budgeting-for-digital-marketing/

7. http://www.bighospitality.co.uk/Business/BigHospitality-s-2012-look-back-Catering-for-diners-with-special-dietary-needs-and-the-London-2012-Olympics

8. http://www.zeromomentoftruth.com/

9. http://www.epsilon.com/news-and-events/press-releases/2012/q3-2012-north-america-email-trend-results-more-brands-rely-trigg

10. http://www.flowtown.com/blog/dine-and-dish-are-social-media-and-food-the-perfect-pairing

11. http://techtalk.currys.co.uk/press-releases/table-for-two-becomes-table-for-10-as-brits-show-increased-appetite-for-social-media-at-the-dining-table/

12. http://www.designcouncil.org.uk/about-design/Measuring-design/

13. http://kantarmedia-tgigb.com/2011/01/24/social-networking-on-the-move-over-50s-accelerating-faster-than-their-younger-counterparts/

14. http://searchengineland.com/study-43-percent-of-total-google-search-queries-have-local-intent-135428

15. http://allthingsd.com/20120827/big-years-for-instagram-and-pinterest-bust-up-the-social-networking-charts/

About the Author

Susanne Currid is a digital marketing strategist and coach who specialises in helping businesses to successfully engage with their customers through social media.

She first fell in love with the digital world whilst producing award-winning CD-ROMs in the mid-90s. As the Internet revolution gathered pace, she established herself as a digital expert producing marketing initiatives for start-ups and big brands including Sony Music, Channel 4 and Cushman & Wakefield.

In 2010, as Global Head of Online Marketing, Susanne was part of the team that helped Patersons Global Payroll win a raft of international business awards including T-Mobile Fast Growth Company of the Year. In 2011, Susanne founded The Loop Digital Communications Ltd where she now provides strategic social media consultancy and coaching to restaurant & bar operators and other fast-growth businesses.

Susanne is a regular speaker at events and on radio. She also blogs at www.the-loop.com/blog.

Follow Susanne on Twitter: @susanne_currid

For more advice and articles on marketing from Susanne Currid visit: www.the-loop.com

Printed in Great Britain
by Amazon.co.uk, Ltd.,
Marston Gate.